WHY?
BECAUSE.
BECAUSE
WHY?

Because
I want some
answers!

NATIONAL GEOGRAPHIC
WASHINGTON, D.C.

NATIONAL
GEOGRAPHIC
KiDS

WHY?

ANIMALS

99+ AWESOME ANSWERS FOR CURIOUS KIDS

JULIE BEER

WHY
DO **FLAMINGOS** **STAND** ON **ONE LEG?**

WHAT
IS THE **WORLD'S** **SLIMIEST ANIMAL?**

DO
CATS REALLY ALWAYS **LAND ON THEIR FEET?**

WHY
DO **FIREFLIES LIGHT UP?**

Are you bursting with questions? Well, you've come to the right place! Welcome to *Why? Animals,* a book jam-packed with straightforward answers to all the animal-related questions you've ever thought to ask—and even some you haven't! You'll learn why cheetahs have tear marks, why koalas hug trees, why dogs wag their tails, and why cats' pupils look like slits. From wild animals to domestic, living animals to long-extinct ones, you'll get answers to an amazing array of fantastic animal questions, like How do lizards walk on water? Can animals have accents? And just why were *Tyrannosaurus rex*'s arms so teeny-tiny?

And there's more. Take trivia-filled quizzes to test your animal expertise!

You'll also hear from in-the-field experts, such as a conservationist who offers tips on how we can help protect animals in the rainforest. And you'll meet a wildlife photographer who explains how taking photos of endangered wild animals can actually save them. Bonus—he also gives advice on how to take professional photos of your pets.

By the end of this book,
your brain will be as full of answers as a blue whale's stomach is of its favorite food. (What—and how much—does Earth's biggest animal eat, you wonder?) And speaking of questions, here's another one: Why do chameleons change color? Turn the page, and you'll find out!

WHY do CHAMELEONS change COLOR?

Chameleons are little magicians. These lizards don't have a forceful bite, they aren't poisonous, and they don't move very fast. What they can do is change color—which is their greatest form of defense against predators. But don't expect chameleons to match every environment they're in. If you set a chameleon alongside a chessboard, its skin isn't going to look like checkered squares. Their skin closely resembles the natural environment they live in, so they simply make adjustments to their hues to blend in even better.

Chameleons that live in trees are generally green, and ones that live in deserts are often brown. Chameleons pull off their shade shift with the help of two layers of cells on top of their skin that contain tiny, light-reflecting crystals. Chameleons can shift these crystals to reflect light differently, and then—voilà!—their color changes right before your very eyes.

A CHAMELEON'S TONGUE **IS ABOUT** TWICE AS LONG **AS THE** LENGTH OF ITS BODY.

Chameleons can turn DRAMATIC COLORS to attract a mate or to defend their turf.

THE WORLD'S SMALLEST CHAMELEON **CAN FIT ON** THE TIP OF A MATCHSTICK.

WHY do ELEPHANTS have such GOOD MEMORIES?

If someone tells you that you have a memory like an elephant, consider it a compliment. Not only do elephants have the largest brain of all land animals, but the part of their brain that processes memories is also larger and denser than in most other animals—including humans. Older female elephants seem to have the best memories—which can literally be a lifesaver to their herd. During a drought at Tanzania's Tarangire National Park, researchers observed that the herds with the oldest female elephants had the greatest chance of survival. Why? The matriarchs had lived through a similar drought 30 years earlier and remembered where they had found alternative food and water sources. They guided their herd to the same spot. For elephants, the reward for recollection may take some time, but it is well worth the wait.

ELEPHANTS CAN RECOGNIZE THEIR OWN REFLECTION IN A MIRROR.

An **AFRICAN ELEPHANT'S BRAIN** is three times larger than a human's.

No Map?
No Problem.

Sea turtles don't have any problem remembering directions. Born on beaches all over the world, logger-head sea turtles return to the same location they were born decades later to lay their own eggs. How do they do it? They use Earth's magnetic field. Coastlines have a unique magnetic field, or signature, that the sea turtles remember and then locate when they are headed home to nest.

Dung beetles look skyward to find their way. The insects—which roll balls of dung, or poop, and then lay eggs in them—use the moon as a reference point to travel in a straight line at night. What happens when the moon isn't visible? Although the insects' eyes can't see individual stars, they can see clusters of stars, like the Milky Way galaxy. Scientists think they use the concentration of light as a substitute for the moon.

WHY do SNOW MONKEYS take BATHS?

Japanese macaques, also known as snow monkeys, elevate taking a bath to a full spa treatment. For decades, these monkeys have been observed soaking in hot springs during the frigid winters on Japan's main island of Honshu. What's with the steamy soak? These animals know where to go to keep toasty. When the region's temperatures drop below freezing and several feet of snow cover the ground, the hot springs' hot-tub–like temperatures keep the chill in check. While the monkeys soak, they often take turns grooming one another—a way to keep clean but also to bond. A study found that these group gatherings help them cope with the stress of trying to warm up and likely increase their survival. If you're a snow monkey, it turns out bath time may also be the key to a longer life.

ON LAND, SNOW MONKEYS SOMETIMES HUDDLE IN GROUPS OF UP TO 20 TO SHARE BODY HEAT AND STAY WARM.

Of all nonhuman primates, SNOW MONKEYS live in the COLDEST CLIMATE.

FEMALE SNOW MONKEYS WITH THE REDDEST FACES HAVE A HIGHER SOCIAL STATUS.

WHAT is the SLIMIEST ANIMAL?

If you can fill a bucket with slime in less than a second, you win the slimiest animal award. Slime is a hagfish's superpower. The 18-inch (46-cm)-long eel-like fish goes into serious defense mode when threatened, releasing a sticky mucus, or slime, and tiny fibers that sting and clog predators' gills. And if that doesn't work, the hagfish has a backup move: It can squirm out of its predator's grasp by tying itself in a knot, thanks to the fact that it lacks bones. But hagfish are also predators themselves. They have an extendable tongue with two rows of sharp teeth on it, plus a hooklike fang to snag worms and other invertebrates that live on the seafloor. And the hagfish has even more quirky characteristics: It is the only animal with a skull but no spinal column; it has three hearts that can beat for hours without oxygen; and it has eyes but is almost blind.

HAGFISH SNEEZE IF THEIR NOSTRILS FILL WITH SLIME.

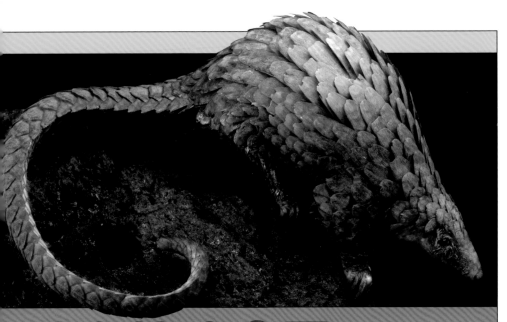

WHAT is the SCALIEST ANIMAL?

A pangolin's TONGUE can be LONGER than its ENTIRE BODY.

Pangolins may look like reptiles, but they're mammals—in fact, they're the world's only truly scaly mammal. Pangolins are covered in scales from head to tail, except for their hairy bellies. The scales look like a suit of armor, and they act like one, too. When startled, pangolins cover their heads with their front legs and roll into a ball, exposing sharp scales on their tails to use as a defense. The scales are thin and light but have sharp edges. Baby pangolins are born with soft scales that harden after a few days. Pangolin scales are made of keratin—the same material as human fingernails. Even though they don't have any proven medical value, the scales are used in traditional Asian medicine, making pangolins one of the world's most heavily poached animals.

WHY do ANIMALS SHED their FUR?

When winter is around the corner, it's out with the old and in with the new for animals that shed their coats. Trading in that summer coat for a thicker one keeps animals toasty during harsh winter weather. But growing a new coat can serve another purpose: camouflage. Cold-climate animal species—like the arctic hare and arctic fox—often grow whiter fur to help them hide in the snow.

Even though dogs evolved to become our domestic companions thousands of years ago, their coats reflect their wilder days. It doesn't matter what climate they live in; genetics determines the type of coat your dog has and how much fur it sheds. Some dog breeds, like Siberian huskies, have a thick undercoat and shed a lot. Pugs have less fur and don't shed as much.

DURING HIBERNATION, BEARS SHED **NOT ONLY** THEIR FUR **BUT ALSO** THEIR FOOTPADS.

In the spring, **ARCTIC MUSK OX SHED up to EIGHT POUNDS (3.6 kg) of FUR.**

THE ARCTIC FOX DOUBLES THE LENGTH OF ITS COAT ON ITS BELLY DURING WINTER.

WHY do SWARMS of GNATS CHASE ME?

Nothing says summer like riding your bike through a cloud of gnats. Gnats, which are in the same family as mosquitoes, hover in large groups. They especially thrive in hot, rainy weather (like a summer rainstorm) and feed on grasses. Like mosquitoes, gnats are fond of humans and are particularly attracted to fruity and sweet smells. Scents from soaps and shampoos may draw them in, and so might body heat and moisture, like sweat. So if you walk (or ride) through a swarm, you might find a few tagalongs that like your smell.

ONLY MALE GNATS SWARM.

FUNGUS GNATS, which feed on fungi in potting soil, often INFEST INDOOR HOUSEPLANTS.

Strength in Numbers

Gnats aren't the only animals that swarm. As a group, these animals make an impressive display.

DESERT LOCUSTS

Most of the time, desert locusts hang out on their own in the dry regions of North Africa and South Asia. But sometimes weather conditions force them to find one another. When they come together in a swarm, they transform into a buzzing beast. They turn from tan and green to black and yellow and become aggressive. Desert locust swarms can contain a billion or more locusts, cover an area 1.5 times the size of New York City, and eat 300 million pounds (136 million kg) of crops in a day!

STARLINGS

When starlings gather, they put on a synchronized show. Called a murmuration, tens of thousands of the birds swoop and dive together as one. When one bird changes direction, the others in its immediate area move, too, almost instantly. The movements are often a response to a nearby predator, like a hawk.

RED CRABS

These crabs are serious about hitting the beach! Each year on Australia's Christmas Island, 60 million red crabs make their way from the forest to the sea. They emerge together on the first rainfall of the wet season, usually in October or November, to mate and spawn. The timing of the migration is specific: It is always before dawn, when the high tide is receding during the last quarter of the moon.

I'LL SCRATCH YOUR BACK, IF YOU SCRATCH MINE.

The general rule of the animal world is to stay clear of predators that can attack you. But a few unlikely animal duos have a symbiotic relationship—they rely on each other for help. And in the case of these pairs, it's a win-win all around.

OXPECKER AND RHINO

Red-billed oxpeckers stand on the backs of rhinos and peck at their skin, cleaning off and munching on harmful parasites like ticks. That's a nice perk for the rhino, and the bird benefits from a hearty meal. Oxpeckers also hiss loudly when they spot a potential predator, warning rhinos of the threat.

CLOWNFISH AND SEA ANEMONE

Sea anemones' stinging tentacles are deadly to most small fish, but clownfish snuggle right into them, thanks to a protective mucus on their skin. In return for this hiding place, when other fish come looking to prey on the clownfish, the sea anemone scores a snack.

BARBEL AND HIPPO

Hippos are gentle giants when their fish friend the barbel is around. Barbels feast on hippos' ticks and other skin parasites. There's so much trust in this relationship that hippos open up their mouths to let the fish eat food caught in their teeth!

WHY do OCTOPUSES shoot INK?

Talk about a dramatic exit. When an octopus—or squid or cuttlefish—is scared, surprised, or angry, it produces the perfect diversion to make an escape: ink. The ink is stored in a sac near the octopus's gut until it's ready to release it. And when the need arises, the octopus squirts out the ink, along with some water and mucus. The murky black cloud lingers long enough for the octopus to flee the scene. But it's more than just a smoke screen. The ink contains a compound that can temporarily blind a predator. It also scrambles the predator's sense of taste and smell.

As if those tricks weren't enough, an octopus has one more up its sleeves. The mucus that is released with the ink helps the black cloud hold a shape, often appearing like a silhouette of the octopus and confusing predators as to their prey's whereabouts.

OCTOPUSES have another DISTRACTION TACTIC: They can REMOVE AN ARM and let it wiggle away to CONFUSE PREDATORS.

OCTOPUS INK IS GENERALLY BLACK, BUT SQUID INK IS DARK BLUE.

AN ARTIST USED INK TAKEN FROM A 95-MILLION-YEAR-OLD OCTOPUS FOSSIL TO DRAW A PICTURE OF THE OCTOPUS.

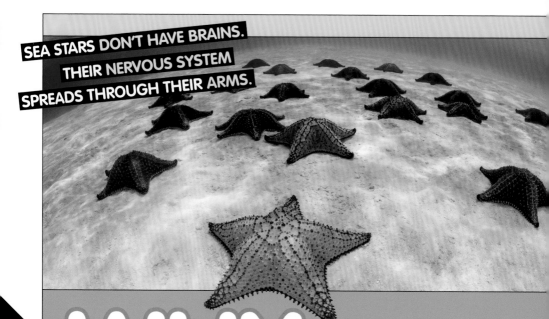

SEA STARS DON'T HAVE BRAINS. THEIR NERVOUS SYSTEM SPREADS THROUGH THEIR ARMS.

WHY are STARFISH now called SEA STARS?

Because they aren't fish! Sea stars are echinoderms, a type of animal closely related to sea urchins and sand dollars. For a long time, these creatures, which live in all of the world's oceans, were called starfish. But over the past 50 years, more and more scientists have put a new spin on their name to accurately describe them. There's still an issue with their moniker, though: Sea stars aren't all star-shaped. The five-armed varieties that look like a star are the most common type, but some, like sunflower and Antarctic sun sea stars, have 20 and even 40 arms! But naming these animals can allow for both accuracy and creativity: The chocolate chip sea star looks like an after-dinner treat, and arctic cookie stars appear practically edible, too, with their delicate pink and white patterns.

A basket star

WHY do LLAMAS SPIT?

Llamas and their alpaca cousins could use a little help with their manners. If they're in a bad mood or feeling threatened, they'll spit—and at quite a distance. They are able to hit their target from up to 15 feet (4.6 m) away. Although llamas rarely spit at people, they sometimes spit at each other in competition for food or to establish dominance. And they will launch a stream when facing an attack from a predator. They also show defiance in other ways: Llamas are used as pack animals, and if they are overloaded, they will sometimes refuse to move until their load is lightened. But llamas can also be very protective. They often adopt a herd of sheep or goats as their own and chase off predators like coyotes. And they have a sweet side: Mama llamas hum to their babies, and their babies hum back.

Llamas can **TELL THE DIFFERENCE** between a **DOG** and a **COYOTE**.

23

WHY are PANDAS BLACK-and-WHITE?

Even though they are black-and-white, pandas are still as eye-catching as brightly colored animals. Their black ears, which stand up straight on top of their head, black arms and legs, black shoulder bands, and black eye patches are a sharp contrast to their white bodies. (One exception is the brown-and-white panda, which gets its coloring from a rare genetic mutation.) Pandas' markings are similar to other pandas', but they are all slightly different, which helps scientists tell the bears apart. It's believed that pandas' black markings help them hide in the forest shade, and their white body markings help them blend in with snow. This is important because, unlike other bears, pandas don't hibernate during winter. A panda's black ears might signal a warning to predators such as leopards. And the black eye patches can be a way for individual pandas to distinguish between one another. And—cuteness alert!—when pandas don't want to appear aggressive, they cover their eyes with their paws.

PANDAS' PUPILS HAVE VERTICAL SLITS LIKE A CAT.

Why Are Pandas Born Pink?

Pandas don't look very panda-like when they're born. For the first few days, pandas have very little fur and their pink skin is exposed. But white woolly fur quickly begins to grow, and within about three weeks their black fur follows, covering up their pink skin.

Pandas sometimes ROLL— rather than WALK— to get somewhere FASTER.

A panda cub is about 1/900th the weight of its mama bear, roughly the size of a stick of butter. This makes them one of the smallest newborn mammals when compared to the size of their mother. Besides being tiny, newborn panda cubs are also blind, deaf, and unable to crawl. For the first several months of their life, they are dependent on their mom for everything. But by six months old, they start to munch on bamboo, and by 18 months, they're usually ready to head off on their own.

WHY do DOGS EAT GRASS?

ONE STUDY FOUND THAT 68 PERCENT OF DOGS EAT GRASS DAILY OR WEEKLY.

Do you ever let your dog out in the yard for a romp, and instead of chasing a ball, she starts munching on the lawn? Even though this behavior seems a little odd—and not very tasty!—veterinarians say it's not unusual for dogs to eat grass. There are different theories as to why dogs graze grass. It's not because they're looking for something that's missing in their dog bowl: Commercial dog food contains all the vitamins and minerals that most dogs need. One theory is that grass can soothe an upset stomach. But again, studies show that the majority of dogs aren't sick before they eat grass, and the majority don't get sick after. The likely reason dogs eat grass: They think it tastes good! These are the same pets that chew on dirty socks, after all.

CHOCOLATE **IS THE** HUMAN FOOD **THAT MAKES** DOGS SICK MOST OFTEN, A STUDY FOUND.

A GOLDEN RETRIEVER **SET A** WORLD RECORD **BY FITTING** SIX TENNIS BALLS **IN HIS** MOUTH.

WHY do PIGS ROLL in MUD?

If anyone ever tells you that you sweat like a pig, don't be offended. Pigs don't sweat—or more specifically, they don't have functional sweat glands. This means they don't regulate their temperature by sweating like some other animals do. So how do pigs cool off? By rolling in the mud! Mud takes longer than water to evaporate from their bodies, keeping them cool for extended periods of time. Although humans might take mud baths at spas to pamper their skin, pigs muddle in puddles for more practical reasons: The mud acts as a sunscreen, protecting pigs' sensitive skin from burning. And it even serves as a barrier to mosquitoes, ticks, and other parasites. Scientists think that pigs inherited their love of a good soak. They are distant relatives of hippos, which also delight in a muddy dip.

A PIG'S SQUEAL IS AS LOUD AS A CHAIN SAW.

Pigs Dig Dirt!

For several thousand years, humans turned to pigs to help find a buried treasure of sorts—truffles! Truffles, sought-after delicacies for gourmet dishes, are mushrooms that grow about six inches (15 cm) underground next to trees. They produce a hint of scent that the human nose can't detect. But pigs can sniff out the truffles and dig them up with their snouts.

A domestic pig digs for truffles.

There was just one problem: When the pigs found the favored fungi, they gobbled them up! That's why in Europe, Northern California, and the Pacific Northwest, trained dogs have replaced pigs as truffle hunters. Super-sniffing dog breeds, like the Lagotto Romagnolo, are pros at finding truffles, but have no interest in tasting the treasure.

A full-grown domestic PIG can WEIGH as much as a GRAND PIANO.

Black truffles

DO CATS

really always **LAND**

on their **FEET?**

DON'T TEST THIS OUT ON YOUR CAT. Just because cats land on their feet doesn't mean they can't get hurt.

Have you ever noticed that no matter how drowsy your cat is, if he is bumped off the couch, he appears to always plop right onto his feet? And if he gets shooed off the kitchen counter? Drops to his feet again. Cats have an amazing ability to turn themselves around quickly and typically land on their paws, thanks to something called a righting reflex. As soon as cats are in a free fall, an automatic response kicks in and they instinctively rotate both the front and back ends of their body in opposite directions at the same time. This twisting—a motion made possible by a flexible spine— allows a cat to orient its feet toward the ground. (Cats need about 12 inches [30 cm] of space to have enough time to twist and land properly). And house cats aren't the only acrobats—wild cats land on their paws, too.

DOMESTIC CATS **CAN** JUMP SIX TIMES **THEIR** OWN HEIGHT.

LEOPARDS can JUMP 10 FEET (3 m) straight up.

SAY WHAT?!

SNOW LEOPARDS **CAN** LEAP **AS FAR AS** 50 FEET (15 M) IN ONE STRIDE.

WHY do HYENAS LAUGH?

It's not usually fun and games when a hyena laughs. Spotted hyenas, which live throughout Africa and parts of Arabia and India, make a vocalization that sounds like a person hysterically laughing—sometimes described as high-pitched *hee-hee-hee*'s. But spotted hyenas don't make this sound when they're playing. They generally laugh when they are being chased or under attack, especially if there's a fight over food. Scientists think that when a hyena is threatened, the laughing sound is a cue for the aggressor to back off. But laughing can also be an accidental invitation. The noise can alert nearby hyenas that something is going on, causing them to come investigate—and perhaps join the quest to snag a free meal.

Even though they are quick to get in food fights, hyenas are social. They live in groups, called clans, of up to 80 members, which females lead. They break off into small packs to hunt, but once an attack has been made, it's every hyena for itself to get the spoils.

spotted hyena

Hyenas EAT and DIGEST BONES.

HYENAS LOOK LIKE DOGS BUT ARE MORE CLOSELY RELATED TO CATS.

What Made That Sound?

Some animals make pretty unexpected noises. Match the animal to the sound they sometimes make.

CHEETAH

BRUSHTAIL POSSUM

PIRANHA

WALRUS

DESERT RAIN FROG

GIRAFFE

FEMALE MOUNTAIN LION

Chirp

Bark

Whistle

Hum

Scream

Revving Car

Squeak, like a dog toy

ANSWERS: Cheetah: Chirp, Brushtail possum: Revving car; Piranha: Bark, Walrus: Whistle, Desert rain frog: Squeak, like a dog toy; Giraffe: Hum, Female mountain lion: Scream

WHY do SEA OTTERS FLOAT in SEAWEED?

Sea otters spend most of their lives in the ocean—hunting, eating, and sleeping in the water. And because they're such social animals, they often hang out together in a group called a raft. When sea otters snooze, they float on their backs. And to keep from drifting too far out to sea, they sometimes float in kelp forests. They use the giant seaweed, which grows as tall as a three-story house, as an anchor. They also cling to one another by holding paws. Mama sea otters have to keep a very close eye on their pups so they don't float away. Pups have the ability to float from the moment they're born, so when a mama goes hunting, she wraps her pup in seaweed or puts it on a rock or the shore while she grabs a bite. Besides playing babysitter to sea otter pups, kelp forests also supply food for sea otters. Sea otters love to munch on sea urchins, which feed on kelp. Urchins can wipe out kelp forests if their populations aren't checked, so the otters' appetite provides an important balance to the ecosystem.

A SEA OTTER STORES A ROCK IN A LOOSE FOLD OF SKIN UNDER ITS ARM AND PULLS IT OUT TO CRACK OPEN HARD-SHELLED PREY, LIKE CLAMS.

SAY WHAT?!

SEA OTTERS ARE THE ONLY MARINE MAMMAL THAT CAN LIFT AND FLIP OVER BIG ROCKS ON THE OCEAN FLOOR.

SEA OTTERS HAVE THE DENSEST FUR OF ANY MAMMAL.

WHAT
IN THE WORLD?

A bald eagle may sometimes **attack an osprey, another bird of prey, in flight,** forcing it to drop its food so the eagle can eat it.

Bald eagle nests are up to **10 feet** (3 m) **wide** and **20 feet** (6 m) **deep.**

Bald eagles are **born** with **brown head feathers** that don't **turn white** for five years.

BALD EAGLE

WHY do SEALS LIE on the BEACH?

Barrel-shaped and bulky, seals certainly don't look like they're made for life on land, but in fact, some species, like harbor seals, spend about half their time out of water. With their stubby front flippers, seals haul themselves onto beaches, rocky shores, and ice to rest, give birth, and soak in the sun. They also come to land to molt. Seals lose their fur once a year, and because fur grows faster when they're onshore than in the water, they spend more than their usual amount of time on land to regrow their fur during this season. Less time in the water means they also don't eat as much. Part of a family called pinnipeds that includes sea lions and walruses, seals don't always need to be wet like other marine mammals. It's in their DNA: Millions of years ago their ancestors—weasels and bear-like animals—lived on land.

SEALS CAN SLEEP WHILE HOLDING THEIR BREATH UNDERWATER.

A NARWHAL can have TWO TUSKS jutting from its head, though this is RARE.

WHAT do NARWHALS
use their TUSKS for?

Narwhals get their nickname, unicorns of the sea, for their trademark corkscrew tusk that can grow up to 10 feet (3 m) long. But because the animals, which live in northern Arctic waters, are so elusive, scientists didn't have a clear idea of what exactly the tusk is used for—until 2017. Using a drone, researchers tracked a pod of narwhals and caught them on camera using their tusks to hit codfish with a quick movement. This stunned the fish long enough for the narwhals to gobble them up. But scientists think the tusk is even more useful. Weighing more than 22 pounds (10 kg), the tusk is also used as a pick to break through Arctic ice, a weapon in fights, and—because the tusk is covered in thousands of nerve endings—the perfect projection to sense their location.

WHY do ROOSTERS CROW in the MORNING?

To most people, a rooster crowing means one thing: The sun is coming up! Roosters have an internal clock, which helps them know when it's sunrise. And a rooster's crow, which is its way of singing, is part of its daily routine. Most animals have internal clocks, also known as circadian rhythms. These daily cycles are why even if your alarm isn't set, your body wakes up around the same time every day—and you get tired around the same time at night. But a rooster's crow is about more than just timing. It's also a way for him to claim his territory. A study found that the highest-ranking rooster in an area crows first at dawn. His crow is a signal to other nearby roosters that they better not trespass onto his territory. Lower-ranking roosters have to wait their turn to cock-a-doodle-doo, following the top rooster's daily song.

ROOSTERS ARE A SIGN OF GOOD LUCK IN PORTUGAL.

ROOSTER-CROWING CONTESTS **are held in GERMANY and BELGIUM, with** competitions including longest crow.

Test Your Farm Animal Smarts

How well do you know your farm animals? Take the following quiz and check your answers below:

1. A baby goat is called a _____ .
a. joey
b. pup
c. kid
d. lamb

2. The average horse's heart is the size of a _____ .
a. tennis ball
b. softball
c. basketball
d. beach ball

3. True or false: Barn owls, which sometimes live in the rafters of barns, hoot.

4. How much milk can a dairy cow produce every day?
a. 3 gallons (11 L)
b. 10 gallons (38 L)
c. 25 gallons (95 L)
d. 40 gallons (151 L)

5. True or false: You can tell the gender of a turkey based on its poop.

6. One pound (.45 kg) of sheep's wool makes _____ .
a. 10 miles (16 km) of yarn
b. 1,000 yards (914 m) of yarn
c. 100 feet (30 m) of yarn
d. 10 feet (3 m) of yarn

ANSWERS: 1. c; 2. c; 3. False (They don't hoot; they scream.); 4. c; 5. True; 6. a

WHY do WALRUSES have such BIG TEETH?

Imagine carrying around a pair of teeth that are as long as a skateboard and weigh 12 pounds (5.4 kg) each! A walrus's tusks are its signature look, but they also serve multiple purposes. Males and females each have a pair of tusks, and they use them to haul themselves out of the water and onto ice. Considering walruses weigh up to 3,000 pounds (1,360 kg), these teeth are pretty strong. Sometimes walruses even rest in the water by hooking their tusks onto blocks of sea ice to stay afloat. They also use them as an ax to open breathing holes in the ice from the water below. And males use their tusks when fighting to maintain their territory. Tusks grow throughout a walrus's entire life and are such a part of the animal's identity that its species name is Latin for "tooth-walking seahorse."

IF THREATENED, A MOTHER WALRUS WILL PICK UP HER CALF WITH HER FLIPPERS AND HOLD IT TO HER BODY, DIVING INTO THE WATER TO AVOID PREDATORS.

SAY WHAT?!

WALRUSES SQUIRT WATER **ON THE** OCEAN FLOOR **TO** UNCOVER BURIED MOLLUSKS.

The HAIRS on a WALRUS'S MUZZLE are as SENSITIVE as HUMAN FINGERS.

WHY do DOGS WAG their TAILS?

When you meet a dog on the side-walk and it's wagging its tail, it means the pup is happy to see you, right? Not necessarily. A dog's tail can offer telltale clues to humans and other dogs as to how the animal is feeling. If a dog's tail is lowered or between its legs, it can mean the pup is feeling scared or anxious. A tail held high could mean it's curious about something. Or a tail held high, moving with tiny, high-speed wags, can be a threatening display, suggesting the dog is ready to fight. An energetic wag from side to side, accompanied by a bow or a few licks, can be a friendly hello. If a dog is wagging its tail in a circle, it usually means it is especially excited—the kind of greeting you get when you walk in the door after a week at sleep-away camp.

A dog that has a POSITIVE FEELING about something WAGS ITS TAIL more to the RIGHT SIDE of its body, a study showed.

Decoding Your Dog's Body Language

DOGS MAY TILT THEIR HEADS TO THE SIDE TO HEAR A PARTICULAR SOUND MORE CLEARLY.

A tail wag doesn't tell you everything. Other signs can indicate how your dog is feeling. He might not be able to talk, but your dog's body language speaks volumes. A dog with ears up but not forward means it's relaxed; ears forward might mean it is listening to something; and ears forward and pointed out might mean it is on edge. A dog with its ears back can mean it is fearful or agitated. A dog's face is another giveaway: If its nose and forehead are smooth, it means it is relaxed or curious. A wrinkled nose or curled lips can mean it is aggressive.

fearful or agitated

relaxed or alert

listening

aggressive

WHY do CHEETAHS have TEAR MARKS?

Don't worry, those streaks on a cheetah's face aren't stains from crying. A cheetah's distinctive tear marks, which begin at the corner of its eyes and continue down to its mouth, may improve its hunting skills. In fact, the word "cheetah" comes from the Indian Sanskrit word *citraka,* which means "distinctly marked." Researchers think the black streaks might help reduce the sun's glare so that cheetahs can see their prey better. So, why don't other big cats have tear marks? They don't hunt during daylight like cheetahs do. Cheetahs, which hunt solo, have adapted to hunt during the day to avoid competing with larger predators like lions and leopards, which hunt mostly at dawn and dusk. Cheetahs' eyes also sit higher on their heads than on the other big cats, allowing them to look over a vast area like the African savanna.

AFTER IT CAPTURES PREY, A CHEETAH HAS TO REST TO CATCH ITS BREATH BEFORE EATING.

CHEETAHS are the only big cats that **CAN TURN IN MIDAIR** during a hunt **TO CATCH PREY.**

SAY **WHAT?!**

A CHEETAH'S CLAWS AREN'T RETRACTABLE, WHICH GIVES IT EXTRA TRACTION WHEN ON THE RUN.

WHY do ANTS like SUGAR?

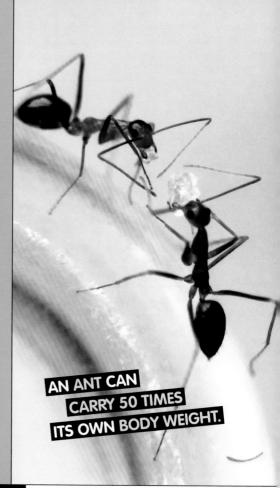

Have you ever opened a cabinet and found a trail of ants headed straight for the sugary treats? Some types of ants have a bit of a sweet tooth because sugar has something the ants need—energy! But a study found that ants living more than 60 miles (100 km) from the ocean prefer salty snacks over sugary ones. All ants (and animals) need salt for their nerves, muscles, and water balance. Ants that live farther from the ocean's salt water likely have less access to salt, and will show more of an interest in salty foods than ants that live near the ocean. Ants find their way to a food supply—whether sugar or salt—by following a trail. When an ant finds food, it secretes an invisible chemical trail as it returns to the nest. Other ants follow this chemical trail, and release their own chemical to keep the trail strong.

AN ANT CAN CARRY 50 TIMES ITS OWN BODY WEIGHT.

WHY do FLIES like POOP?

Female flies choose to lay their eggs in some pretty stinky spots. Prime real estate for a housefly's eggs is decaying material (like leftovers in a trash can or compost heap), dead animals (like roadkill), and a fresh mound of poop. Poop offers everything a fly needs for its eggs to hatch: It's moist but not too wet, and it's squishy. The best poop is fresh and hasn't dried out. Females lay up to 500 eggs in batches of 75 to 150 over three or four days. (Flies only live about 15 to 25 days, so they need to move quick.) These eggs have to stay moist or they won't hatch. That's why you're more likely to see flies land on fresh dog poop than on a pile that hasn't been picked up in a few days!

Flies have TINY HAIRS or bristles on the BOTTOM of their FEET, which is how they can WALK UPSIDE DOWN on ceilings.

WHY were PREHISTORIC CATS SO BIG?

Talk about big kitties. American lions weighing as much as about 500 pounds (227 kg) roamed the Americas 13,000 years ago, attacking bison, giant ground sloths, and young mammoths. *Smilodon fatalis,* a saber-toothed cat that lived in the Western Hemisphere at that time, weighed up to 600 pounds (272 kg) and had seven-inch (18-cm)-long canine teeth. A Pleistocene jaguar was jumbo-size—about 15 percent larger than today's jaguar. Prehistoric cats lived during a time when animals were oversize and classified as "megafauna." For 35 million years after dinosaurs went extinct, mammals kept growing. The largest mammals were plant-eaters and were able to eat more—and, over time, grow larger—because they no longer had to compete with dinosaurs for vegetation. And the extra-large carnivore cats kept the herbivore megafauna populations in check.

But beginning about 125,000 years ago, megafauna started disappearing. Scientists think that was in part because of climate change and also because humans over-hunted them. After the Ice Age, the era of megafauna was over. Today's mountain lions that roam the same range as the prehistoric American lions are about half their size.

Saber-toothed cat *Smilodon fatalis* could OPEN ITS MOUTH almost TWICE AS WIDE as today's big cats can.

Why Did Early Humans
Draw Lions on Cave Walls?

Humans have a long history with big cats. A cave in France has paintings on the walls created by hunter-gatherer Paleolithic people more than 30,000 years ago that show a number of animals, including 16 lions in pursuit of bison. Researchers think the paintings—which are known as the Gallery of Lions—could represent stories, or they could have been part of a ritual. Because the lions are shown as symbols of power and their faces were often drawn with a humanlike profile, researchers think the animals were likely well respected.

Replica of Gallery of Lions

EXCAVATORS have found more than 2,000 **SABER-TOOTHED CATS** buried in the **LA BREA TAR PITS** in California, U.S.A.

JUST THE FACTS:
ANIMAL MYTHS BUSTED

Some animals are misunderstood—and even get a bad reputation—based on rumors that just aren't true. It's time to settle the score and get to the bottom of some common animal myths.

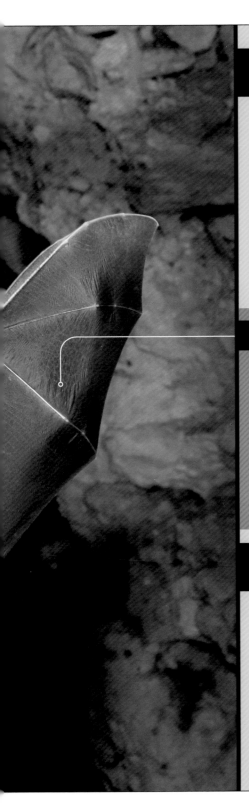

MYTH! OSTRICHES BURY THEIR HEADS IN THE SAND.

The flightless African bird, which stands up to nine feet (2.7 m) tall and weighs up to 350 pounds (159 kg), does sometimes hold its head near the ground to feed on plants or tend to its nest. From a distance, that could look like its head is buried—and is perhaps how this myth got started.

MYTH! BATS ARE BLIND.

Bats' flying style can be zigzagged and unpredictable, perhaps creating the myth that they can't see well. In fact, larger bats' vision is three times better than ours. But a bat's true sensory superpower is hearing. Bats navigate and find food by using their large ears to pick up on sound waves that bounce off objects.

MYTH! THE COLOR RED MAKES BULLS ANGRY.

In one stage of a bullfight, a matador uses a red cape to entice a bull to charge, but the color of the cape isn't what makes the bull respond. In fact, bulls are partially color-blind and cannot see the color red. What makes the bull agitated is likely the waving motion of the cape.

53

WHY do CAMELS have HUMPS?

Contrary to what you might think, a camel's hump (or humps, depending on the type of camel) is not filled with water. It stores up to 80 pounds (36 kg) of fat, which the camel uses when it doesn't have access to food and water sources. When a camel's fat stores are depleted, its hump droops. But once it rests and refuels—a camel can drink 30 gallons (114 L) of water in 13 minutes—the hump goes back to normal. Needless to say, camels are pretty hard-core: They can walk up to 100 miles (161 km) in the desert without drinking water. And they rarely sweat, even in temperatures over 120°F (49°C), which helps them conserve water. In the winter, when water is scarce, camels get moisture from desert plants. Thanks to their tough, flexible lips, camels can eat thorny plants—and even cacti—that other animals avoid.

A CAMEL SOMETIMES GREETS ANOTHER CAMEL **BY** BLOWING **IN ITS** FACE.

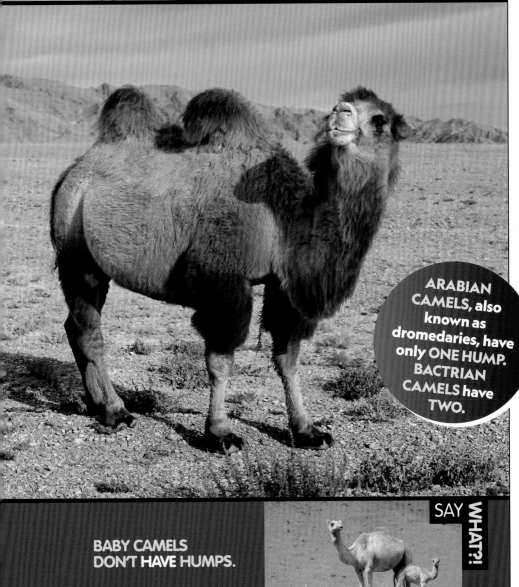

ARABIAN CAMELS, also known as dromedaries, have only ONE HUMP. BACTRIAN CAMELS have TWO.

BABY CAMELS DON'T **HAVE** HUMPS.

SAY WHAT?!

WHAT kind of animals did people in ANCIENT CIVILIZATIONS keep as PETS?

Humans have looked to animals for companionship for thousands of years. Wolves were domesticated and became pets—what we recognize as dogs today—when humans were hunters and gatherers at least 20,000 years ago. Helpful partners in keeping rodents away from grains, cats first lived with people 8,000 years ago. In ancient Greece and Rome, dogs were companions but also protectors, keeping homes safe from thieves, and livestock safe from wild animals. Some ancient civilizations kept even more exotic pets. Ancient Egyptian pharaohs not only kept dogs to help them hunt and guard, but also had monkeys and falcons as pets. Monkeys provided entertainment, and falcons helped them hunt. In ancient China, royalty kept small dogs, called sleeves. They gained their name because these companions could be carried around in their caretakers' sleeves. But they didn't just stay stashed in shirts: If they felt their owner was threatened, they would pop out and bark furiously in defense.

PUGS WERE A FAVORITE BREED OF CHINESE RULERS MORE THAN 2,000 YEARS AGO.

Artwork depicting ancient Egyptians with their pet monkey

TWO THOUSAND YEARS AGO, THE COLIMA PEOPLE OF WESTERN MEXICO MAY HAVE KEPT HAIRLESS DOGS AS PETS.

Match the Ancient Civilization With the Sacred Animal

People have revered animals for thousands of years, giving them special status in society based on spiritual beliefs and mythologies—sometimes associating them with a god or worshipping them as divinities. Can you pair the animal with the ancient civilization that revered it?

CAT | TIGER | RED-CROWNED CRANE | JAGUAR | OWL

A: ANCIENT CHINA | B: ANCIENT EGYPT | C: ANCIENT GREECE | D: ANCIENT KOREA | E: ANCIENT AZTEC

WHY do SQUIRRELS BURY their NUTS?

No, they're not planning a scavenger hunt. Bushy-tailed squirrels scurry around hiding nuts and seeds to prepare for winter, when food is less available. But burying and recovering their stash is more complicated than you'd think.

A study found that squirrels only find and eat 26 percent of the nuts they bury. Not only that, squirrels can lose as much as a quarter of their stockpile to other animals that find it first, like birds. Luckily, any nuts or seeds that remain underground aren't all a loss. For instance, some acorns that squirrels bury eventually sprout and turn into oak trees, helping forests flourish. And squirrels don't survive on nuts and seeds alone. They eat roots, leaves, eggs, and even insects and caterpillars. Squirrels compete with one another for food, but their biggest rival is woodpeckers, which are looking for the same food and nesting sites.

Ruby-throated hummingbirds **WEIGH LESS** than a **PENNY.**

WHERE do HUMMINGBIRDS GET their NAME?

Hummingbirds aren't songbirds, so where does the "hum" in hummingbird come from? Their wings! The wings of some hummingbird species flap up to 100 times a second. This flapping makes a low buzzing, or humming, sound. Hummingbirds can hover in the air while they gather nectar from flowers, and they can fly backward, sideways, and even upside down. The rufous hummingbird flaps its wings more than most others: It migrates all the way from Alaska, U.S.A., to Mexico and back again. But their wings aren't the only thing that's fast about hummingbirds. Their heart can beat 1,000 times a minute! And their heart-to-body-size proportion is five times larger than a human's. It takes a lot of energy to keep that heart beating and those wings flapping. As a result, hummingbirds drink up to 10,000 calories from 1,000 flowers every day.

WHY do some ANIMALS GLOW in the DARK?

Those lights aren't coming from an undersea dance party. More than three-quarters of marine animals are bioluminescent, which means that they produce their own light or carry bacteria that glow. Depending on the animal, they glow to attract prey, warn off other animals, or communicate with one another. When crystal jellyfish are disturbed, more than 100 light-producing organs around their bell glow green.

Female anglerfish, which live in the sunless depths of the ocean, don't produce their own glow, but use glowing bacteria to bait prey. The female fish has a long dorsal fin tipped with bacteria whose light attracts small fish, which don't notice the needlelike teeth behind the wiggling lure until it's too late. Lanternfish have a line of glowing lights on the sides of their bodies from head to tail that they can turn on and off. Scientists believe they

flash their lights as a way to communicate with one another in the dark deep sea. Some also have a light on the tip of their heads that helps them see where they are swimming!

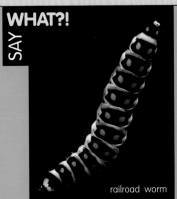

railroad worm

railroad worm
with glowing spots

FEMALE RAILROAD WORMS HAVE GLOWING SPOTS ON THEIR SIDES THAT LOOK LIKE THE WINDOWS OF A TRAIN LIT UP AT NIGHT.

LANTERNFISH make up **60 PERCENT** of all **DEEP-SEA FISH** living in the world's oceans.

HAWAIIAN BOBTAIL SQUID GLOW BLUE, MIMICKING THE MOONLIGHT FOR CAMOUFLAGE AT NIGHT.

WHY do MOSQUITOES BITE MY FEET?

Mosquitoes are serious ankle biters. These insects that feast on the blood of humans and other warm-blooded animals inject saliva into their victims with a hollow tube called a proboscis. Some of their favorite areas to target on humans? Feet and ankles. It turns out that mosquitoes are drawn to the stinky smell of feet. When they get up close to investigate, they often attack. Mosquitoes are also attracted to heat and lactic acid—two things your body produces when you sweat. So if you're exercising in your favorite old running shoes, your ankles are mosquito magnets. Some people are extra irresistible to mosquitoes—and it has nothing to do with their scent. A study found that people with type O blood attract mosquitoes twice as often as people with type A blood. Ask your doctor what your blood type is so you'll know if you need to be extra alert to swat mosquitoes away!

How to Tell Mosquitoes to Buzz Off

Here are some ways to avoid becoming a mosquito's next meal.

The **HUMMING SOUND** mosquitoes make comes from the **FLAPPING** of their **WINGS**, which beat up to 500 times a second.

COVER UP

Spraying on insect repellent and wearing clothing that covers up your skin are good ways to keep mosquitoes from getting too close. If a mosquito can't land on your skin, it can't bite you!

SLEEP BUG FREE

If you're camping or sleeping outdoors in a place that has lots of mosquitoes, cover your sleeping area with a bug net. At home, make sure that open windows have screens on them so mosquitoes can't swoop inside.

AVOID STANDING WATER

Mosquitoes breed in still water, so make sure to help your parents empty any watering cans and kiddie pools to discourage mosquitoes from gathering.

AVOID MOSQUITOES' DINNERTIME

Mosquitoes are especially active during dawn and dusk. So watch out for them when doing outdoor activities during these peak biting hours.

WHY do
some **ANIMALS** carry their **BABIES** in a
POUCH?

Some animals have a built-in pocket. Female marsupials—like kangaroos, wallabies, opossums, and koalas—give birth to babies (called joeys) that are tiny and not quite done forming. So the baby crawls into the mother's pouch to nurse and stays there for weeks or months, depending on the animal species. The inside of the pouch is hairless and lined with sweat glands that release substances to protect the baby from illnesses and parasites. But how can a joey get in and out of the pouch? The mama marsupial is able to open and close the pouch using a special muscle. This is a safe and comfy place for the baby to grow until it is ready to be in the outside world. Then the joey hops out of the pouch and stays close to its mom until it's time to venture out on its own.

OLDER OPOSSUM BABIES RIDE ON THEIR MOTHER'S BACK AS SHE HUNTS FOR FOOD.

GREEN RINGTAIL POSSUMS ONLY LEAVE THE TREE CANOPY IF A NEIGHBORING TREE IS TOO FAR TO REACH.

WOMBATS, A TYPE OF MARSUPIAL FROM AUSTRALIA, HAVE CUBE-SHAPED POOP!

SAY WHAT?!

WHY don't ANIMALS get HUNGRY when they HIBERNATE?

Our tummies rumble when dinner is an hour later than usual. Imagine not eating for a whole winter! Some animals do just that when they hibernate. During hibernation, animals conserve energy to survive tough weather conditions or lack of food. Different animal species hibernate different lengths of time, and they don't technically "sleep." Rather, their metabolism is reduced to less than 5 percent of normal. In the case of dwarf lemurs, their heart rate goes from 300 beats a minute to fewer than six. And they can go 10 minutes without taking a breath! Because hibernating animals are in energy-conservation mode, they don't have their usual daily needs—like eating and drinking. Weather determines when animals go into hibernation and when they come out of it, so hibernating season varies a little bit from year to year.

TO PREPARE FOR WINTER HIBERNATION, DORMICE DOUBLE THEIR NORMAL SIZE DURING SUMMER.

A whale's ESOPHAGUS—the tube that connects the mouth to the stomach—is only FOUR INCHES (10 cm) WIDE.

WHAT ANIMAL has the BIGGEST APPETITE?

It takes a lot of food to fill the belly of the blue whale, the largest animal on Earth. This beautiful creature can grow up to 100 feet (30 m) long and weigh up to 200 tons (180 t). Its tongue alone weighs as much as an elephant! But the bulk of a blue whale's diet is made up of little shrimplike animals called krill. They're only about two inches (5 cm) long, so a blue whale has to eat several million krill—up to 7,900 pounds (3,600 kg) worth—every single day to get enough energy to swim through the ocean.

Baby blue whales are big eaters, too! When they're born, they weigh three tons (2.7 t)—about half the size of an elephant—and by drinking their mother's fatty milk, the whales gain about 200 pounds (90 kg) every day during their first year. By seven months old, they are the size of four elephants!

WHAT
IN THE WORLD?

As the world's fastest eater, it can find and **devour an insect** in under **half a second.**

STAR-NOSED MOLE

The mole's tentacles are **five times more sensitive** than human fingertips.

The star-nosed mole's nostrils are ringed with **22 sensitive tentacles** used to explore its environment.

T. rex had strong legs, but it WASN'T a FAST runner—it could only move at 12 miles an hour (19 km/h).

WHY were TYRANNOSAURUS REX'S arms so SHORT?

T. rex has all the makings of a ferocious and fierce predator ... except for those little arms. Why did this 40-foot (12-m)-long, 12-foot (3.7-m)-tall dinosaur with a powerful tail and crushing jaw filled with 60 serrated teeth have such proportionately puny arms?

Scientists have proposed multiple theories: The arms might have helped the dinosaur push itself up from the ground—or perhaps their arms were once bigger, but the fossils we've discovered are the ones that evolved to be smaller. New research offers another idea: T. rex's arms adapted to a shorter length to slash prey at close range. Their four-inch (10-cm)-long claws could make a pretty deep wound if the prey were close enough. But really, short is all a matter of perspective: T. rex's arms were three feet (0.9 m) long! They just look small on its extra-large body.

WERE
DINOSAURS the BIGGEST
animals to ever LIVE?

It depends on how we define "biggest." No animal that ever lived weighed as much as today's blue whale. At 200 tons (180 t), it is more than 25 times heavier than a *T. rex*! The longest dinosaur, *Patagotitan mayorum,* was about 120 feet (37 m)—around 20 feet (6 m) longer than a blue whale, but it was much lighter. It tipped the scales at 70 tons (64 t), only about one-third the weight of a blue whale. One record *Patagotitan mayorum* can claim: It was the largest animal to walk on land. It weighed about 12 times more than today's largest land animal, the African elephant. When a cast of the dinosaur's skeleton was made for a museum in New York City, it couldn't fit in the room where it was being displayed, so its head peeped out into the next gallery space!

With its neck stretched tall, *PATAGOTITAN MAYORUM* was as tall as a seven-story building.

CAN a GROUNDHOG really PREDICT the arrival of SPRING?

February 2 is Groundhog Day in the United States, where people gather in Punxsutawney, Pennsylvania, to watch the behavior of a groundhog named Punxsutawney Phil. According to the annual tradition, which began in 1887, if Phil sees his shadow, there will be six more weeks of winter. If he doesn't, an early spring is on the way. Groundhogs have pretty regular hibernation patterns, and around February 2 the males come out of their burrows and claim their territory. So groundhogs aren't really weather predictors; they're just following their natural instinct. As far as accuracy goes, data gathered between 2010 and 2019 showed that Punxsutawney Phil was correct about 40 percent of the time.

GROUNDHOG DAY IS RELATED TO CANDLEMAS, A MIDWINTER GERMAN HOLIDAY WHEN A GROUNDHOG FORECASTS WINTER WEATHER.

WHEN GROUNDHOGS HIBERNATE, THEIR HEARTBEAT GOES FROM 80 BEATS A MINUTE TO FIVE.

GROUNDHOGS ARE ALSO KNOWN AS WOODCHUCKS AND WHISTLE PIGS.

DOES
COUNTING SHEEP
help you go to
SLEEP?

Having a glass of warm milk, taking a bath, and counting sheep—these are all common recommendations for ways to catch some z's. Sure, warm milk and a bath can be comforting and relaxing, but how does envisioning sheep jumping over a fence help you go to sleep? As it turns out, it really doesn't. Sleep researchers conducted a study of people who have a hard time falling asleep and tried different sleep-aid techniques to see how they responded. Researchers asked them to count sheep or to imagine a relaxing scene, like the beach. The people who thought about something relaxing fell asleep 20 minutes faster than the sheep counters.

Orangutans can **BUILD A NEST** in three minutes.

Weird Animal Sleep Habits

These animals have a unique way of hitting the hay.

KEEPING COZY

Orangutans don't just make their bed every day, they make a brand-new bed. High up in a tree, orangutans find a sturdy branch and then start bending and breaking branches, weaving them together to make a bed frame. Then they add smaller branches as the mattress. Some orangutans even braid branches over their heads to make a roof. The following day, their bed building begins again.

HALF-AWAKE

Think how much more playtime you'd have if you didn't have to sleep! Dolphins can stay awake for at least five days straight. Their brains have adapted so that half can be perfectly alert when the other half is asleep.

KEEPING AN EYE OUT

Fruit bats always have an eye on things, even when they're asleep. Hanging upside down, a fruit bat keeps one eye closed and tucked under its wing while the other eye peers out to keep a careful watch for predators.

WHY do LIONS have MANES?

Holding the title of king comes with an eye-catching accessory: a mane. Male African lions have thick manes around the face and neck that quickly set them apart from the females. But what's the purpose of this majestic face-framing fluff? None of the other big cats, like tigers and leopards, have manes, and the Asiatic lion, which lives in India, has a shorter mane than African lions. Female African lions, which don't have manes, do most of the hunting for the pride, and they hunt on the savanna. Males tend to hunt from vegetation to keep their prey from noticing them, though their manes don't likely help with camouflage. The purpose of a mane seems to be more about social status than functionality. Male lions with longer, darker manes are more popular with females than lions with shorter, lighter-colored manes.

SAY WHAT?!

WHAT?!

SAY

MALE LIONS **DON'T START** GROWING MANES **UNTIL** THEY ARE ABOUT ONE YEAR OLD.

MALE TSAVO LIONS, WHICH LIVE IN KENYA, HAVE THIN MANES OR NONE AT ALL, WHICH KEEPS THEM COOLER IN THE HOTTER CLIMATE.

LION'S MANE JELLYFISH **ARE NAMED FOR THEIR** HAIRLIKE TENTACLES, WHICH LOOK LIKE A LION'S MANE.

SAY WHAT?!

WHAT mammal SLEEPS the SHORTEST amount of TIME?

The biggest land animal on Earth is also the shortest sleeper of all mammals. Wild African elephants sleep less than two hours a day and can even go two days without any sleep at all. When they do catch some z's, they sleep standing up more often than lying down. Grazing animals like elephants tend to sleep less than animals that hunt and eat a big meal in one sitting, because grazers need to spend as much time as they can eating to meet their daily nutritional needs. Giraffes and horses also only need a few hours of sleep a night. Small mammals, such as mice and squirrels, process their food quickly and can spend more time—about 12 to 14 hours a day—snoozing.

CATS SLEEP ABOUT 12 HOURS A DAY.

DO animals DREAM?

When your cat is sleeping the day away, is she dreaming about the mouse that escaped her paws? It's hard to know if animals dream— or at least dream like we do— because they can't tell us about their dreams when they wake up from a slumber. Scientists observe animals' behavior while they sleep and see if their sleeping brains work like ours. A study of cats revealed that they seem to see images during their sleep, based on how their bodies moved. A study of brain activity in rats showed that while they were sleeping, they retraced a maze they had run through earlier in the day. What we don't know is whether animals remember their dreams when they wake up.

WHY do CROCODILES shed TEARS?

If someone asks you if you're crying crocodile tears, they're suggesting that you're pretending to be sad. The phrase goes back centuries to a European fable that says crocodiles cry while eating their prey because they are faking remorse. It turns out, there really is something to crocodiles crying, but it has nothing to do with them feeling guilty about catching their latest meal. Crocodiles—and their relatives, alligators and caiman—hiss and huff while eating, which forces air through their sinuses and out their eyes. This buildup of pressure causes them to tear up. Sometimes their eyes even bubble! Crocodiles aren't the only weepers: All vertebrates, including reptiles and birds, produce tears, which helps keep the eyes moist, clears out any debris, and protects against infection. So, before you think you see a critter crying over something sad, remember that humans are the only animals believed to shed emotional tears.

CAIMANS, A RELATIVE OF CROCODILES, CAN GO HOURS WITHOUT BLINKING.

A crocodile has a THIRD EYELID that it uses to PROTECT its EYES during an ATTACK.

WHEN SEABIRDS DRINK OCEAN WATER, THEY GET RID OF THE SALT THROUGH A SPECIAL GLAND NEAR THEIR EYES.

AN ISLAND TO THEMSELVES: ASTOUNDING ANIMALS OF MADAGASCAR

Madagascar, the fourth largest island in the world and located about 250 miles (402 km) east of southern Africa, is home to some of the world's most unique animals. Almost 90 percent of the plants and animals living on Madagascar can't be found anywhere else on Earth.

HOW DID THE ANIMALS GET THERE?

About 165 million years ago—when dinosaurs roamed Earth—Madagascar slowly broke off and drifted away from Africa. But most of the land animals that live on the island today didn't evolve from the animals that lived there when it split off from Africa. Instead, they likely caught a ride on some vegetation that drifted over.

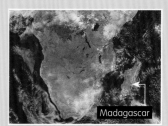

Madagascar

NO ROOM FOR THE OVERSIZE

Madagascar is also missing many large mammals that live on the African mainland, including elephants, lions, and antelope. The only large African mammal that lived on the island was the dwarf hippopotamus, which is now extinct. Humans have only lived on Madagascar for about 2,000 years.

ONE OF A KIND

Ring-tailed lemurs are not only unique because they live exclusively on Madagascar—they also know how to make a statement: They have long tails with 13 alternating black-and-white bands, or rings, on them. Because they have little fur on their bellies, they face the sun in a "yoga position," soaking in the rays to warm up.

DO ANIMALS have ACCENTS?

Yes, some animals sure do!
The majority of animals are born "speaking" the same species' language, no matter where they call home. That's because speech is imprinted in their genetic code. But a few species have ways of communicating that are specific to their region. For instance, some songbirds, like black-capped chickadees and white-crowned sparrows, combine sounds in such unique and specific ways that researchers can identify in which U.S. state they live by listening to their songs. They can even pinpoint in which area of a particular city the birds live. In San Francisco, California, researchers identified more than 10 dialects in white-crowned sparrows. A sparrow at Golden Gate Park sounds different from one a few miles away at Golden Gate Bridge. Some whales also have regional accents. Sperm whales in the Caribbean use different clicking patterns, which are a form of echolocation, from those living in the Pacific Ocean. Researchers think these regional accents help these mammoth mammals identify which waters they swim from and also reinforce family bonds.

A BLUE WHALE'S SONG **CAN** TRAVEL **MORE THAN 600 MILES (1,000 KM)** UNDERWATER.

SCIENTISTS who study gray wolves can **IDENTIFY** individuals based on their **UNIQUE HOWL.**

SAY **WHAT?!**

CITY BIRDS USE A HIGHER PITCH THAN COUNTRY BIRDS OF THE SAME SPECIES TO HELP REDUCE ECHOES THAT BOUNCE OFF BUILDINGS, A STUDY FOUND.

WHY are some RABBITS' eyes RED?

Rabbits with red eyes and white coats have a genetic mutation called albinism. There's no other difference between them and other rabbits except that they lack the ability to make melanin, the main pigment that gives animals their fur, eye, and skin coloring. But looks are deceiving: A rabbit's iris reflects light, and normally the light is reflected from the color of the eye. Because an albino rabbit doesn't have any color, it reflects light from its blood vessels, which are red. That's what gives an albino rabbit its red-eyed appearance. White rabbits with red eyes are quite rare in the wild, because being all white—except when living in snowy conditions—is a disadvantage for blending in with the landscape in a rabbit's natural habitat. But white rabbits are popular pets, so they have been deliberately bred, making them a common sight.

Rabbits can TURN THEIR EARS 180 DEGREES, which helps them listen in all directions for predators.

Albino rabbit

WHITE TIGERS AREN'T ALBINO—THEY ARE A RARE TYPE OF BENGAL TIGER.

Eye Spy

Can you match the animal with their eye-catching peepers?

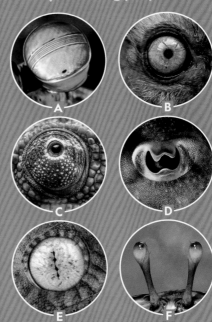

A

B

C

D

E

F

BLUE-EYED LEMUR
Other than humans, blue-eyed lemurs are the only primates with blue eyes.

PEACOCK MANTIS SHRIMP
With eyeballs that move independently on movable stalks, nothing gets past a peacock mantis shrimp.

CHAMELEON
Chameleons can rotate their eyes separately to look at two different objects at the same time.

LEAF-TAILED GECKO
It's hard not to look twice at the leaf-tailed gecko's marbled eyes, which have a series of dots for pupils.

FIDDLER CRAB
Fiddler crabs get a better view with eyes that sit high on top of their stalks.

CUTTLEFISH
With a W-shaped pupil, cuttlefish eyes are wow worthy.

ANSWERS: Blue-eyed lemur: B; Peacock mantis shrimp: F; Chameleon: C; Leaf-tailed gecko: E; Fiddler crab: A; Cuttlefish: D

WHAT is the LOUDEST ANIMAL?

One of the biggest noisemakers on land is the suitably named howler monkey, which lives in Central and South America. A group of howler monkeys' calls can be heard three miles (5 km) away. The males are able to crank up the volume thanks to their large throats and vocal chambers. And their howl sends a clear message—stay away from our turf! But the animal that makes the most racket is one that most humans have never heard. A sperm whale makes vocalizations underwater that reach 230 decibels and can be heard by other sperm whales hundreds, and maybe even thousands, of miles away. That level of decibels, if heard above water, is louder than a military jet at takeoff. But water is denser than air, so to a human's ear, a sperm whale's underwater call sounds more like 174 decibels. (And even that is still loud enough to burst eardrums!)

MALE KAKAPO BIRDS **ALTERNATE BETWEEN** DEEP BOOMING CALLS **AND** LOUD WHEEZING SOUNDS **TO ATTRACT FEMALES.**

MALE COQUI FROGS, which are native to Puerto Rico, compete for the loudest CROAK—which can be as loud as a JACKHAMMER.

MALE CICADAS **MAKE A BUZZING** SOUND **THAT'S LOUDER THAN A** SUBWAY TRAIN, **BUT FEMALES ARE SILENT.**

WHY do HERMIT CRABS CHANGE SHELLS?

Hermit crabs know when it's time for a home upgrade. These crabs have mostly soft bodies, so they need shells to protect them from predators and any pokes and prods that come with living in sandy or muddy marine water. Because they are born without shells, they must go in search of abandoned ones. As their bodies grow, they need to replace their shells when they get too tight. So they go looking for new ones. But interestingly, if a crab finds a shell that doesn't fit, it doesn't just walk away and keep shopping. Scientists have observed that a hermit crab will wait by the shell, and then as more crabs show up, they line up in order of biggest to smallest. Once a crab fits in the empty shell and moves in, the other crabs continue to look for their own perfect fit, swapping their shells with one another.

Hermit crabs are SOCIAL, living in GROUPS OF 100 or more.

WHY do CHINCHILLAS take DUST BATHS?

A pet chinchilla

Take a bath in dust? Now how does that get you clean? Chinchillas have some of the softest fur of all animals, so clearly they know what they're doing. We think of getting clean by jumping into a tub full of water, but chinchillas keep their coats clean with dust—from volcanic ash or clay—which removes moisture, oil, and dirt. Chinchillas live at elevations of 16,400 feet (5,000 m), and rely on their thick fur to stay warm. When under attack, chinchillas can do a "fur slip," instantly shedding a clump of fur and leaving a predator with a mouthful of fuzz. And they aren't the only dust bathers. Some birds, like wrens and sparrows, take to dirt to clean up. Dust soaks up extra natural oil in their feathers and also prevents parasites, like lice.

Chinchillas can JUMP a distance of up to SIX FEET (1.8 m).

IS CORAL a PLANT or an ANIMAL?

Coral looks like a plant, but it is an animal! Technically called coral polyps, these marine invertebrates are related to sea anemones and jellyfish, but it's easy to confuse them with a plant for a number of reasons. Coral polyps permanently attach themselves to the ocean floor, similar to how plants take root in soil. But the polyps don't make their own food the way plants do. Instead, they use their tentacle-like arms to grab food and push it into their mouth. Coral polyps can live individually or in large colonies that make up an entire reef structure. They use minerals from the seawater to build a hard skeleton of limestone that protects their soft bodies. The thousands of species of coral also provide food and habitat for 25 percent of the world's marine life.

STAGHORN CORAL, WHICH LOOKS LIKE DEER ANTLERS, CAN GROW NEARLY AS TALL AS AN ADULT HUMAN.

CORAL POLYPS have CLEAR BODIES with WHITE SKELETONS—they get their color from tiny algae that live on them.

Plant Look-alikes

Coral isn't the only one that leaves you guessing if it's a plant or animal.

SEA ANEMONE
Sea anemones are extra confusing because they're named after a plant—the anemone flower. Anemones are usually found attached to rocks on the bottom of the ocean or on coral reefs, where they wait for fish to swim close enough to get caught in their venomous tentacles.

SPONGE
Sponges are the simplest animals on Earth. They don't have tissue or organs. They are fixed to the ocean floor and eat by filtering food through their structures, gathering nutrients and oxygen. Sponges provide a safe habitat for animals like crabs and sea stars.

ORCHID MANTIS
Female orchid mantises eat pollinating insects, so they evolved to mimic flowers that these insects like to visit: orchids. Instead of snacking on a "flower's" nectar, insects become snacks!

ARE JELLYFISH FISH?

Despite their name, jellyfish aren't fish. A fish has a backbone, which makes it a vertebrate. A jellyfish is an invertebrate and is more closely related to coral and sea anemones. Although they're most commonly called jellyfish, marine biologists prefer the term jellies or sea jellies to avoid confusion. Jellies are most famous for the stinging cells in their tentacles that they use to stun and paralyze prey. A jelly eats the prey with its mouth, which is inside its bell-shaped body. Jellies are 95 percent water and lack a brain, heart, bones, blood, and a respiratory system. So how do they know how to get around? Jellies have a basic nervous system that lets them smell, detect light, and respond to things in their environment. But oftentimes they just go with the flow—letting the ocean's currents guide them to their next destination.

BOX JELLYFISH—THE MOST DEADLY JELLYFISH IN THE WORLD—CAN HAVE 24 EYES AND 15 TENTACLES.

A GROUP of JELLYFISH is called a SMACK.

BECAUSE THEY ARE MADE MOSTLY OF WATER, JELLYFISH THAT WASH UP ON LAND ALMOST COMPLETELY EVAPORATE.

WHAT ANIMAL has the STRONGEST BITE?

Watch one snap of a saltwater crocodile's jaws and it's easy to see how this predator has the strongest bite in the animal kingdom. Its crunch comes with 3,700 pounds per square inch (psi) of bite force. Scientists think the croc's bite could rival that of a *Tyrannosaurus rex*! In comparison, humans bite into food with a mere 150 to 200 psi, whereas hyenas, lions, and tigers generate a more impressive 1,000 psi. But a big bite isn't crocodiles' only menacing trait. Saltwater crocs can grow to 23 feet (7 m) long and weigh up to 2,200 pounds (1,000 kg). They lurk along the water's edge just beneath the surface and prey on whatever comes near, from monkeys to water buffalo to even sharks. They use their jaws to grab prey and drag it back into the water until it drowns.

SALTWATER CROCODILES can stay UNDERWATER for an HOUR.

IN AUSTRALIA, SALTWATER CROCODILES ARE CALLED SALTIES.

The Strong Ones

Crocs might have the most ferocious bite, but the following animals have other ways of showing off their strength.

STRONGEST PUNCH

If threatened, the peacock mantis shrimp can snap its claws at speeds of 75 feet per second (23 m/s). That's 50 times faster than the blink of an eye! And those snaps are strong. In aquariums, mantis shrimp have even been known to smash through glass!

Peacock mantis shrimp

STRONGEST GRIP

Don't try to steal the coconut crab's snacks. Its grip is 10 times stronger than ours. Why the need to squeeze? To crack open coconuts, of course— as well as other fruits and nuts.

Coconut crab

STRONGEST KICK

Just because it has fairly spindly legs, don't underestimate an African secretary bird. Its kick has a force five times its body weight—and it delivers its wallop in just 15 milliseconds. Native to sub-Saharan Africa, secretary birds use this move to kill venomous snakes, like cobras, and then eat them.

African secretary bird

WHAT
IN THE WORLD?

Red pandas are more closely **related to raccoons** and **skunks** than to giant pandas.

RED PANDA

Red pandas **climb down trees headfirst,** like squirrels.

Red panda cubs **whistle to get their** mom's attention.

WHAT is a PLATYPUS EXACTLY?

There is nothing typical about a platypus! To start with, this mammal has a bill and webbed feet like a duck, a tail like a beaver, and a body and fur like an otter. Its bill is used to detect electrical signals from underwater prey like worms, insects, and shellfish. Its tail helps with steering underwater, but it also stores fat, which the platypus can live off when food is sparse. This otherworldly animal has another unique characteristic: Male platypuses are venomous. They have a spur on the heel of each of their hind feet that they use in defense and in fights with other platypuses. But that's still not all. Platypuses are one of only two mammals (the other is the echidna) that lay eggs. Females usually produce one to three eggs that hatch into baby platypuses about the size of lima beans.

SAY WHAT?!

BECAUSE THEY DON'T HAVE TEETH, PLATYPUSES SCOOP UP GRAVEL WITH THEIR FOOD TO HELP GRIND IT UP.

WHAT?!

PLATYPUSES HAVE FOLDS OF SKIN THAT COVER THEIR EYES WHEN THEY DIVE UNDERWATER, MAKING THEM UNABLE TO SEE WHERE THEY ARE SWIMMING.

Platypuses STORE FOOD in their CHEEKS while SWIMMING and then eat above water.

WHY are MANATEES called SEA COWS?

Even though manatees live their lives in the sea and cows are strictly land animals, the two have one main thing in common: They both spend a lot of time grazing. Manatees munch on algae, water grasses, and weeds for up to eight hours every day, taking in about 10 percent of their body weight. This constant munching, even if on the bottom of rivers or shallow coastal waters instead of pastures, gave manatees their "sea cow" nickname. Like cows, manatees are mammals, but their closest relatives are elephants. They generally surface about every three to five minutes to breathe, but they are capable of staying underwater for as long as 20 minutes at a time. When a manatee comes up for air, it can replace 90 percent of the air in its lungs with a single breath. In comparison, humans replace only 10 percent!

MANATEES HAVE TO TURN THEIR WHOLE BODY TO LOOK AROUND.

HOW do SEAHORSES SWIM?

Seahorses **DON'T HAVE TEETH** or **STOMACHS.**

With a head shaped like a horse and a curly tail, seahorses aren't built to be Olympic swimmers. To get where it needs to go, this tiny fish uses its dorsal fin and the smaller fins on the sides of its head. It steers itself through the water by flapping its fins at a rate of more than 30 times per second. To move up and down, the seahorse changes the volume of air in a pocket inside its body, which is called a swim bladder. Its flexible tail isn't used for swimming, but rather for anchoring. The seahorse uses it to hold on to grasses and coral to keep from getting swept up in strong currents. Because it isn't quick enough to chase after prey, the seahorse uses its long nose like a vacuum to suck in plankton that floats by.

WHY do my DOG'S HACKLES RISE UP?

Have you ever been on a walk with your dog when he spots another pup coming his way and the hair on his neck and back suddenly puffs up? This raised hair on your dog's hackles is called piloerection. It's an uncontrollable response that is equivalent to when we get goose bumps. When your dog's hackles are up, it can be a sign that he is fearful, startled, or excited. Not all dogs raise their hackles in the same way—their hair can puff up between the shoulders, down the spine, or just above the tail. If you see a dog with raised hackles, it can also mean it is aggressive. If you don't know the dog, it's best to give it some space.

DOGS CURL UP IN A BALL WHEN THEY SLEEP TO PROTECT THEIR VITAL ORGANS.

DOGS don't YAWN only when they're TIRED—they also yawn when BORED or STRESSED.

How to Greet a Dog

No matter how fluffy and cuddly a dog looks, not all dogs are up for snuggles—especially from strangers. Here are some tips on how to safely say hello to a dog you just met:

➤ Walk slowly toward the dog and its owner. Ask the owner if it is OK to pet their dog.

➤ If the owner says no, politely keep walking. It's important to respect what the dog's owner says.

➤ If the owner says yes, before you pet the dog, check for yourself to make sure the dog seems friendly. Are its hackles up? Is its tail between its legs? If so, it's better to take a pass on petting.

➤ If all signs point to a friendly dog, make your hand into a fist with the back of your hand facing up. Slowly extend your hand toward the dog.

➤ Allow the dog to sniff the back of your hand, which is its way of getting to know you.

➤ Give the dog a gentle pet under the chin or chest.

➤ Make sure to thank the dog's owner for the meet and greet!

WHY are POISONOUS animals BRIGHTLY COLORED?

Anchor coral snake

Sometimes colors speak louder than words. For poisonous animals like dart frogs, monarch butterflies, and coral snakes, their bright colors are a visual warning to predators that says, "Don't bite me. I'm dangerous." And generally, the warning works. Most predators of these colorful creatures don't bother to try to take a bite. And for good reason. A golden dart frog is one of the most toxic animals on Earth. It has enough poison in it to kill 10 people. Some animals are more secretive about their coloring. Mildly venomous ring-necked snakes are black on top, but if they are flipped over by a predator, they show their bright orange belly. This is called flash coloration and is meant to temporarily confuse a predator long enough for the snake to escape. Ladybugs, which are harmless to humans, are brightly colored to warn predators, like birds, that they are indeed a poisonous snack.

MONARCH BUTTERFLIES **ARE POISONOUS THANKS TO THE** TOXIC MILKWEED PLANT **THEY** ATE **AS** CATERPILLARS.

POISON DART FROGS **are the** SIZE **of a** LARGE PAPER CLIP.

MIMIC POISON FROGS ARE ONLY MILDLY TOXIC, BUT THEY COPY THE BRIGHT COLORING OF POISONOUS FROGS TO TRICK PREDATORS INTO STAYING AWAY.

SAY WHAT?!

WHY do MARINE ANIMALS eat PLASTIC?

Green sea turtle

Plastic surely can't be tasty to marine animals, but they eat a lot of it—by accident. More than five trillion pieces of plastic float in the ocean, from plastic bags to soda bottles. Some of the pieces are so tiny, you'd have to look through a microscope to see them. Plastic might not look like food to us, but to fish, it can look a whole lot like their natural prey. A plastic bag floating in the water looks like a jellyfish to a sea turtle. And jellyfish are one of sea turtles' favorite snacks. Tiny bits of plastic can look like plankton, which sardines like to gobble up. Plastic can be harmful to their health: It can damage their digestive systems or choke them. Many animals also get tangled up in plastic when they're trying to eat it—or when they're simply swimming by.

How Does Plastic End Up in the Ocean?

Every year, 8.8 million tons (8 million t) of plastic end up in the world's oceans. Researchers estimate that, by 2050, the weight of all the plastic in the oceans will be greater than the weight of all the fish in the oceans.

So how does the plastic get there? A lot of different ways. Trash is washed down storm drains, which eventually lead to the sea. Fishing gear is tossed off boats. Rain, wind, and strong storms can send plastic into waterways that lead to the ocean. And any plastic that we put down the drain—from contact lenses to tiny microbeads found in shampoos and other bathroom products—can eventually find its way into the ocean.

Worldwide, 73 PERCENT of BEACH LITTER is PLASTIC.

IT TAKES 450 YEARS FOR A PLASTIC BOTTLE TO BREAK DOWN AND DECOMPOSE.

WHAT is a RHINO'S HORN MADE OF?

Rhinos are probably best known for their horn—or horns, depending on the species. Javan and Indian rhinos have one horn, and the white, black, and Sumatran rhinos have two. They use them to defend their territory from rivals, to protect their calves from predators, and as a tool to dig for water. The horns grow up to three inches (7.6 cm) a year and can be up to five feet (1.5 m) long. Rhino horns are special, in part because they aren't made of bone, like most animal horns. They are made of keratin, the same protein found in our own hair and fingernails. A rhino's unique horn is also its greatest threat. Poachers illegally hunt rhinos for their horns, which are sold and then used in traditional Asian medicine. Poaching has dramatically reduced rhino populations, but conservationists are working to protect the rhinos that remain.

Black rhino

A GROUP OF RHINOS IS CALLED A CRASH.

A PAIR OF ANTLERS on a typical elk weighs 30 POUNDS (14 kg).

WHAT's
the DIFFERENCE between HORNS and ANTLERS?

Horns and antlers may look similar, but what they're made of and how they grow are quite different. Antlers are found in the deer family and are made entirely of bone. They grow from a bony structure called a pedicle on a deer's head and are at first covered in velvet, a thin layer of fuzzy skin that is worn and scraped off over time. Antlers generally only grow on males (with the exception of reindeer), and they lose and regrow them every year. Horns are different. The insides of most horns are made of bone and are an extension of the skull, which means they are permanently attached. They are covered in keratin, the same material as your fingernails. Generally, horns are found on both males and females in a species—such as goats and gazelles.

HOW CAN I HELP PROTECT ANIMALS IN THE RAINFOREST?

Q&A WITH CONSERVATIONIST ANGELA M. MALDONADO

Q: HOW DID YOU GET INTERESTED IN ANIMALS?

A: I always liked animals, and when I was little and thinking about what I wanted to do when I grew up, I thought I'd be a veterinarian. But later I realized I don't like to see animals suffering, and I don't like blood—and knew it was not for me.

Q: YOU STUDIED PRIMATES IN COLLEGE. WHICH IS YOUR FAVORITE?

A: Woolly monkeys! I rescued a woolly monkey named Matias and I learned to understand the animals' behavior. Woolly monkeys live in big groups—with the older ones and offspring helping take care of each other. They're very patient.

Q: WOOLLY MONKEYS AND MILLIONS OF OTHER ANIMALS LIVE IN THE AMAZON RAIN-FOREST. WHAT ARE THE BIGGEST THREATS TO THEIR HABITAT?

A: There are many: Deforestation to plant crops and activities like cattle ranching; big projects like building water dams, which mean the building of more roads; poaching for the illegal wildlife trade and bush meat (meat from wildlife hunted for people to eat). The Amazon is one big ecosystem and spans several countries, so it is complicated and difficult. But a love for the animals keeps me fighting for the cause.

Q: WHAT IS SOMETHING WE CAN DO TO HELP THE RAINFOREST?

A: Look at what you eat and where it came from. Like palm oil, for instance. Companies are deforesting the Amazon to plant African palms, which are an invasive species. Animals here lose their food and shelter source. Avoiding buying foods with palm oil reduces the demand for it and is one way to help.

Colombian conservationist Angela M. Maldonado's mission is to reduce the illegal wildlife trade in the Colombian and Peruvian Amazon—and to help educate people that no matter where they live, they can have an impact on the Amazon rainforest.

WHY do FIREFLIES LIGHT UP?

FIREFLY LIGHT CAN BE YELLOW, GREEN, OR ORANGE.

Despite their name, there isn't any fire involved in the glow that comes from fireflies as they flash on and off during summer evenings. Their light is actually a chemical reaction that happens in their abdomens. Fireflies—which are beetles, not flies—take in oxygen inside special cells, combine it with a chemical called luciferin, and create light. This type of light is called bioluminescence. Fireflies might light up to warn predators that they aren't tasty, even though some frogs are known to eat so many fireflies that they glow themselves. But the main reason fireflies light up is to find a mate. Each of the 2,000 different firefly species has its own flash pattern, which ensures that they attract mates of the same species. They flash at night so their light can be seen and their signal understood. A few types of firefly species, including the ones found in Great Smoky Mountains National Park, U.S.A., flash in sync, like a string of outdoor lights.

New Zealand's Glowworm Caves

Just as fireflies aren't flies, the glowworms that live in New Zealand's Waitomo Cave aren't worms. They are the larvae of a type of gnat that grows as large as a matchstick and has a glowing blue tail. When the larvae hatch, they spin gooey webs that hang from the cave's ceilings. The bioluminescent larvae cling to the webs, lighting the cave like stars. Insects are attracted to the blue light, and fly in to investigate. They get stuck in the sticky trap, and the larvae get their lunch.

A firefly's **LIGHT** produces almost **NO HEAT.**

Waitomo Cave in New Zealand

HOW big
was the world's
LARGEST
SHARK?

The largest shark to ever swim in the sea would have made a great white shark look like a pip-squeak. *Otodus megalodon*, which went extinct some 3.6 million years ago, was up to 59 feet (18 m) long—three times longer than the largest recorded great white. Megalodon could open its mouth so wide that you could swim into it without even touching its teeth! It had 276 razor-sharp chompers, each of which reached up to seven inches (18 cm) long. It likely hunted dolphins and whales—and maybe other sharks. Just like great whites, megalodon had several rows of teeth, and when one tooth broke off, another would replace it. If that's not intimidating enough, this megashark swam in waters around the globe. How do we know this? Megalodon teeth have been found on every continent except Antarctica.

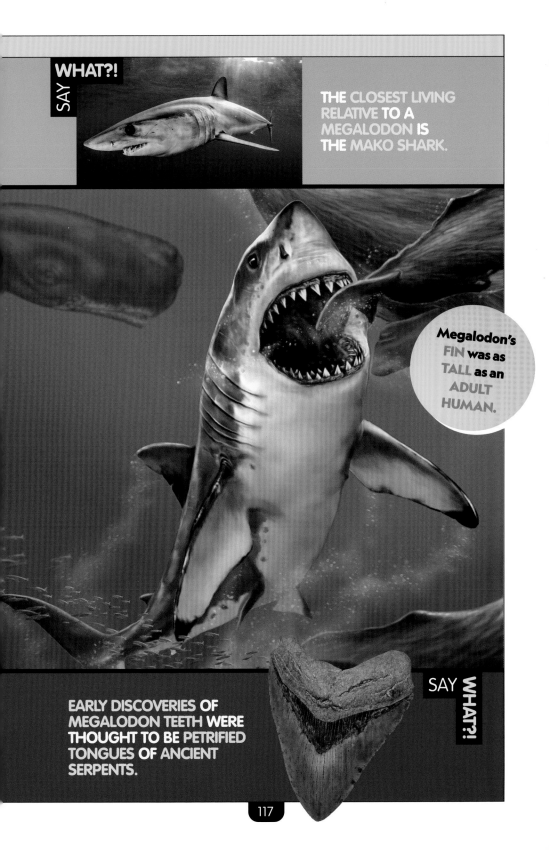

THE CLOSEST LIVING RELATIVE TO A MEGALODON IS THE MAKO SHARK.

Megalodon's FIN was as TALL as an ADULT HUMAN.

EARLY DISCOVERIES OF MEGALODON TEETH WERE THOUGHT TO BE PETRIFIED TONGUES OF ANCIENT SERPENTS.

SAY WHAT?!

WHY do HORSES SLEEP STANDING UP?

You'd think it would be more comfortable to take a nap stretched out on some comfy grass, but horses often doze while standing. They do it for their own safety. It's not easy for a horse to go from lying down to standing up. These awkward moments make them vulnerable to attack from predators, so horses evolved to get some shut-eye while up on all fours. By locking the major joints in their legs, they are able to relax without fear of falling. But horses do settle down for a deep sleep once in a while— about two or three hours a day, often broken up into power naps. When horses get their serious sleep, they often do so when another horse is nearby to look out for potential attackers, such as mountain lions and wolves.

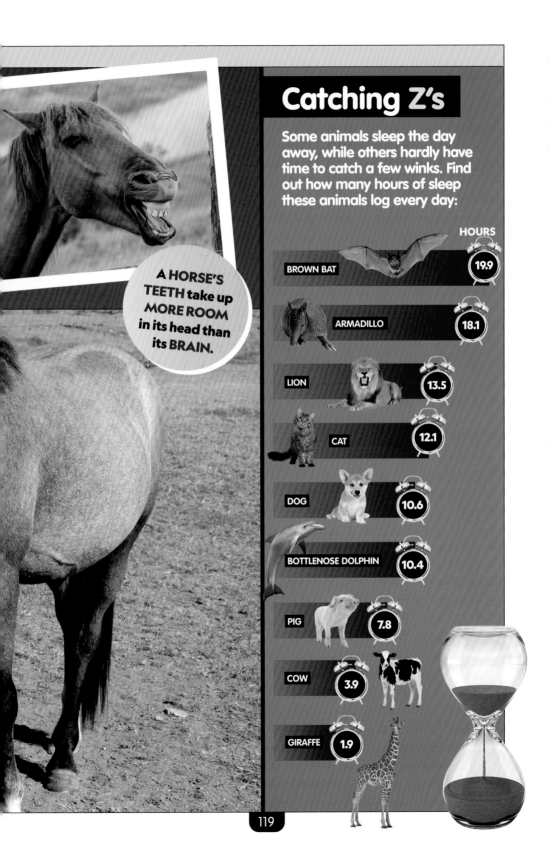

Catching Z's

Some animals sleep the day away, while others hardly have time to catch a few winks. Find out how many hours of sleep these animals log every day:

A HORSE'S TEETH take up MORE ROOM in its head than its BRAIN.

HOURS

Animal	Hours
BROWN BAT	19.9
ARMADILLO	18.1
LION	13.5
CAT	12.1
DOG	10.6
BOTTLENOSE DOLPHIN	10.4
PIG	7.8
COW	3.9
GIRAFFE	1.9

WHY do domestic **CATS' PUPILS** look like **SLITS?**

The pupil is a hole in the eye that lets in light. Our pupils are round. Domestic cats' pupils are a distinctive vertical slit. Interestingly, our pet cats' wild cat cousins—like lions and tigers—have round pupils. Why the difference? A study found that predators like small cats that hunt close to the ground and need to gauge distance before they pounce on prey—or just a mouse-shaped toy—need slit-shaped pupils to see better. Larger ambush predators, like big cats, don't need to see as well and catch prey just fine with round pupils. Although most big cats hunt at dawn and dusk, small cats also move around during the day, so they have to protect themselves from the bright sunlight. The slit pupils are the perfect solution. Cats can close them as much as necessary to prevent too much light from entering their eyes.

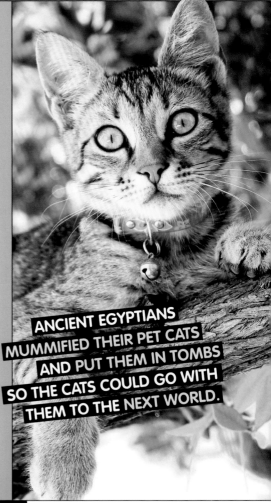

ANCIENT EGYPTIANS MUMMIFIED THEIR PET CATS AND PUT THEM IN TOMBS SO THE CATS COULD GO WITH THEM TO THE NEXT WORLD.

WHY do GOATS' PUPILS look like RECTANGLES?

Goats' peepers certainly make you do a double take. Instead of being round like ours or a slit like that of domestic cats, goats' pupils are shaped like horizontal rectangles. And there's a perfectly good reason for it. When goats are grazing—which is often—they keep their heads down, leaving them vulnerable to predators that may be lurking. Goats need to be able to graze and be on guard at the same time. Their pupils allow for such multitasking. Goats shift their eyes upward while they're eating, and their rectangular pupils remain parallel to the ground, giving them a panoramic view. This means they can have their grass and protect themselves, too. It's no surprise other grazing animals, like sheep, horses, and moose, have also evolved this pupil shape.

GOATS can UNDERSTAND HUMANS' FACIAL EXPRESSIONS.

WHAT
ANIMAL is our closest
RELATIVE?

It's a tie! Chimpanzees and bonobos—both primates—share 98.7 percent of humans' genes. And that 98.7 percent makes us alike in a lot of ways. Members of the great ape family, chimpanzees and bonobos typically walk on their knuckles. However, they are capable of standing and walking upright. And they both use tools. Chimpanzees use sticks to get insects out of nests and use stones to open nuts. They even use leaves like a sponge to soak up water to drink. Bonobos have been seen using a deer's shed antlers to dig up food, and they use long sticks as levers to move rocks. Unlike chimpanzees, bonobos rarely fight with one another and tend to live a more peaceful life. Although chimps and bonobos don't speak like humans do, both have complex ways of communicating through sounds, facial expressions, and gestures.

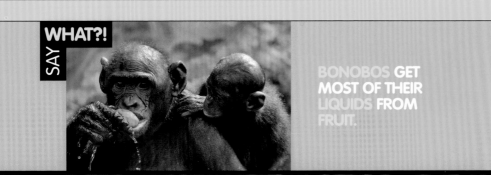

SAY WHAT?!

BONOBOS **GET MORE OF THEIR LIQUIDS FROM** FRUIT.

CHIMPANZEES LAUGH when they **PLAY.**

CHIMPS MIGHT EAT CERTAIN PLANTS TO HELP CURE AN UPSET STOMACH OR HEADACHE.

SAY WHAT?!

WHY do SLOTHS sometimes LOOK GREEN?

Sloths, found in forests of Central America and South America, spend most of their lives in trees, hanging from branches, eating leaves, and sleeping. What they don't do very much is move around. Sloths are the slowest-moving mammals on Earth. They cruise along branches at a rate of six to eight feet (1.8 to 2.4 m) a minute. On an average day, they travel less than half the length of a football field! When they aren't lumbering through leaves, sloths are snoozing. They sleep about 15 hours a day. Life in slow motion allows algae to grow on their fur, which sometimes gives them a green tint. This hue provides extra camouflage in the tree canopy. And their fur is home to more than just algae. Moths, ticks, and beetles nestle in, too. A scientist once found 980 beetles living in a sloth's fur!

SLOTHS sometimes drop from their branches and SWIM IN RIVERS.

A SLOTH'S POOP WEIGHS AS MUCH AS A FIFTH OF ITS BODY WEIGHT.

Sloths Are Green on the Inside, Too.

Sloths certainly get enough servings of greens in a day. During their waking hours, sloths have a one-track mind: food. Luckily, it's all around. That's because sloths only eat leaves. And because they spend almost all their time in trees, they just have to scoot from one branch to the next to grab another handful. How do they wash down all that roughage? They don't! Sloths rarely need to drink water—they get almost all the water they need from leaves. They digest food about as slowly as they move, which means they only need to poop about once every week. The big event of the week involves leaving the tree canopy and climbing down to the forest floor. They usually poop right at the base of the tree and then don't waste any time heading right back up to a branch to begin their eat-sleep cycle yet again.

Three-toed sloth

WHAT was the FIRST ANIMAL on EARTH?

This is a trickier question than you might think! It comes down to two animals: sponges or comb jellies—and scientists have been debating which came first for years. Recent studies point to comb jellies, marine animals that are distant relatives of jellyfish, as being the first animal. They evolved more than 600 million years ago—and are still around today! That's surprising because they are much more complex creatures than sponges, aquatic invertebrates that live on ocean and river floors. It's hard to find evidence of ancient comb jellies because they didn't have bones and left little behind after they died. But scientists were able to do genetic studies on a few rare fossils preserved in farmlands in China to figure out where they landed on the animal family tree—it turns out they were right at the base.

SAY WHAT?!

THE EARLIEST KNOWN MAMMALS **TO** WALK ON EARTH WERE SHREW-SIZE **CREATURES,** LIVING 210 MILLION YEARS AGO.

DRAGONFLIES that lived 275 million years ago were as **BIG AS CROWS.**

THE OLDEST KNOWN ANIMAL **TO** WALK ON LAND **MAY HAVE BEEN** MILLIPEDE-LIKE, LIVING 425 MILLION YEARS AGO.

SAY WHAT?!

WHAT
IN THE WORLD?

The leafy sea dragon uses its **tubelike mouth** as a **straw** to slurp up prey.

LEAFY SEA DRAGON

Leafy sea dragons are **covered in leaflike structures,** which serve as **camouflage** in kelp forests.

In **Australia,** leafy sea dragons are called **leafies.**

WHY do SNAKES STICK OUT their TONGUES?

To sssmell! A snake flicks its forked tongue in and out to detect tiny chemicals in the air, on the ground, and in water. Then it brings its tongue back in to touch two openings on the roof of its mouth. These connect to a sensory center that helps signal if there's something good nearby to eat. A snake's tongue can even tell whether its next meal is to the right, left, or just up ahead.

A puff adder snake uses its tongue to bait prey. Instead of flicking, it sticks its tongue out and slowly wags it, mimicking an insect, in hopes of attracting toads. When one gets too close, the adder quickly strikes—and lunch is served.

White-lipped island pit viper

Rat snake

Top Super Tasters

Snakes aren't the only animals that have good taste. Check out how these creatures use their spectacular sense.

FLIES

House fly

Flies have extrasensitive hairs around their mouthparts and feet that gather information to help them decide whether something is tasty. So when a fly lands on your sandwich, you might find it annoying, but from a fly's point of view, it's just giving your sandwich a taste test!

CATFISH

Yellow bullhead catfish

Catfish have tantalizing tasting abilities. The yellow bullhead catfish is covered from head to tail in more than 175,000 taste buds. (Human tongues have around 9,000 taste buds.)

OCTOPUS

An octopus tastes from an arm's length. Its taste receptors are on its tentacles' suckers. This comes in handy for the octopus, which can hide in a crevice but extend one or more of its eight arms to investigate if something delicious is swimming by.

Coconut octopus

All snakes have FORKED TONGUES, but not all lizards do.

PIGS

With those distinctive snouts, it's easy to imagine that pigs have a good sense of smell. But a sense of taste? Even though pigs are known for eating just about anything, they are super tasters. Pigs have almost twice as many taste buds on their tongues as we do!

Piglet

When dogs get human attention, they make more FACIAL EXPRESSIONS, a study found.

DOES my DOG UNDERSTAND what I SAY?

Yes ... but it depends how you say it. If you've trained her, your dog likely knows to sit when you say "sit." And she probably knows a few important phrases, like, "Do you want a treat?" or "Time for a walk!" But how you're saying your words is as important as what you're saying, a study found. Scientists in Hungary discovered that dogs process speech much like humans do—with a certain part of the brain dedicated to a word's meaning and another part dedicated to the tone of our speech, or how our words sound. When you tell your dog to sit, you probably always use the same serious tone. But if you tell your dog to sit in a singsong voice, she's more than likely not going to know what you're telling her to do. So if she tries to sneak your pizza slice off the table, make sure to use a firm "No!"

SOME PARROTS WEIGH AS MUCH AS A HOUSE CAT.

DO PARROTS really TALK?

Only two animals on Earth can produce human language: humans and birds. Birds, including parrots, ravens, crows, magpies, and mynahs, are masters at mimicking speech and other sounds. These birds hear a sound and imitate it. A zookeeper once found magpies mimicking his call to the chickens at feeding time. The magpies were so convincing that the chickens came running for their meal. But do these crowing copycats know what the words mean? Not really. They are very clever at understanding when to say words, though. For instance, a parrot might say "Hello" when people walk into a room, but only because it is imitating what people do when they walk in. Although your pet parrot might seem like a great conversationalist, he's really just an expert at echoing your words.

WHY do FLAMINGOS STAND on ONE LEG?

Scientists aren't entirely sure, but they have a few ideas. Flamingos often rest by standing on just one leg for a long period of time. The other leg is tucked up under its feathers. One thought is that standing on one leg helps them regulate their temperature: They can have one leg in the water and keep the other warm, then switch. It's also been suggested that alternating their standing leg reduces exposure to parasites and fungus. Or, surprisingly, it could be that flamingos are more balanced when they stand on one leg. Scientists studied young flamingos at a zoo in Atlanta, Georgia, U.S.A., and discovered that the ones that rested on one leg swayed less than the ones that stood on two. The scientists think that flamingos' joints have a "locked" position that helps keep the birds firmly in place when resting on one leg. This yoga-like move doesn't even take practice!

SAY WHAT?!

FLAMINGOS RUN ON THE WATER'S SURFACE FOR A FEW STRIDES BEFORE THEY TAKE FLIGHT.

FLAMINGOS GET THEIR ORANGE-PINK COLOR FROM THE BRINE SHRIMP THAT THEY EAT.

The YOLKS of flamingo eggs can be PINKISH in color.

135

DO ANIMALS DANCE?

Some animals know how to dance to the beat of their own drum. Pigeons bob their heads, male peacock spiders do a courtship dance, and your dog might even be trained to hop in a circle. But scientists say the ability to give it a whirl isn't dancing. Dancing, they say, is a spontaneous response when an animal moves to a beat, trying to match their body movements to the music. They can't be trained to do it, and they can't copy a human who is dancing in the room with them. And when the music changes, the animal can't follow the new beat. (In other words, it needs to know more than one move.) Scientists say the only animals besides humans that are capable of a spontaneous response to music are parrots and Asian elephants. One cockatoo (a type of parrot) named Snowball became an online sensation for his ability to dance to a beat—at least part of the time.

To impress females, the **MALE RED-CAPPED MANAKIN BIRD** slides back and forth on a branch, which looks like the **"MOONWALK"** dance.

Animal Show-Offs

These animals know how to get attention!

BLUE-FOOTED BOOBY
Male blue-footed boobies show off their webbed blue feet for all to see. To impress females, they kick their legs up in a high-step strut. Females are more attracted to the bluest feet.

MANDRILL
It's impossible not to do a double take when you see a mandrill, a type of monkey. Considered one of the most colorful mammals, mandrills have bright blue and red faces—and they get even brighter when they are excited.

PEACOCK
Male peacocks aren't subtle about seeking females' attention. They unfold their train of feathers—which can be as much as 60 percent of their body length—and display it proudly. Females are more attracted to the males with the biggest and brightest blue and green iridescent feathers.

WHY do RAMS BUTT HEADS?

OLDER RAMS SOMETIMES FILE DOWN OR BREAK OFF PIECES OF THEIR HORNS TO GET A BETTER VIEW OF PREDATORS.

Talk about a headache. Bighorn sheep rams, or males, use their horns as status symbols and as a way to show other males their dominance for mating rights. They flick their tongues, kick one another, and then engage in what rams do best: They crash into each other at high speeds. First they rear up on their hind legs, and then they charge at speeds of up to 20 miles an hour (32 km/h) and butt and lock horns. This can go on for hours until one gives up and walks away. How do they avoid brain injury? The rams have evolved extra-thick skull structures that help protect them, and scientists think the horns themselves absorb some of the blows. It's a good thing: Researchers found that the force of two rams crashing heads was 10 times greater than two football players crashing helmets.

WHY do RABBITS THUMP their FEET?

Rabbits don't make much noise, so when they want to make a statement, they use their feet! When rabbits thump a back foot, they are usually reacting to danger that they have seen, smelled, or heard. Rabbits will thump one or both back feet on the ground and then generally run for cover—although some remain in place until they sense the danger has passed. Thumping can also be a rabbit's way of expressing its annoyance. It might not feel threatened, but if it is unhappy about a situation, a thump will say it all. And when a rabbit has something to be happy about? They get happy feet. When rabbits are in a good mood, they "binky"—twisting and kicking in midair. For rabbits, if you're happy and you know it, kick your feet!

Rabbits PURR when they are CONTENT.

ARE ANIMALS as SMART as PEOPLE?

It's hard to be a neutral source for this answer. After all, we humans define what makes an animal smart. But it is generally agreed that humans are the smartest animal, thanks to our quick wits and ability to solve novel problems. But some characteristics place other animals in the highly intelligent category. The first is animals that use tools. Some primates, birds, and even elephants have been observed using objects to accomplish a goal, like getting food. Then there's a test that only a handful of animals have passed: the mirror test. An animal's ability to recognize itself in the mirror—which is called being self-aware—is a long-standing measure of intelligence. Animals other than humans that can see their reflection? Great apes, dolphins, Asian elephants, orcas, and Eurasian magpies.

HUMANS USUALLY PASS THE MIRROR TEST BY ABOUT TWO YEARS OLD.

A crow using a stick to find food

Some **WRASSE FISH** react **AGGRESSIVELY** when they **SEE** their **REFLECTION** in a **MIRROR**, perhaps thinking they see another fish.

Tool Masters

These animals know how to get what they want! Match the animal with the example of how it uses tools:

 SEA OTTER

 GORILLA

 DOLPHIN

 ELEPHANT

 GOPHER

 VULTURE

A
USES A ROCK AS A SPADE TO DIG

B
DROPS STONES ON OSTRICH EGGS

C
USES A BRANCH AS A WALKING STICK TO TEST WATER DEPTH

D
USES STONES LIKE A HAMMER TO OPEN ABALONE SHELLS

E
WEARS A SEA SPONGE ON ITS NOSE TO PREVENT GETTING SCRATCHED

F
MOVES LOGS ONTO ELECTRIC FENCES TO BREAK THE CURRENT

ANSWERS: Sea otter: D; Gorilla: C; Dolphin: E; Elephant: F; Gopher: A; Vulture: B

HOW do LIZARDS RUN on WATER?

Basilisk lizards, which live in tropical forests of Central America, can do the impossible: run on water. Up to 2.5 feet (0.8 m) long (including their tail) and weighing only seven ounces (198 g), basilisk lizards live in trees near the water. If they are threatened or need to chase an insect, they drop from their branch and sprint across the water. What's their secret? Basilisk lizards are flat-footed with long toes on their rear feet that have flaps of skin between them. The flaps open up, increasing their surface area and creating air pockets under their feet, which gives the lizards a lift so they can scamper just above the water's surface. They can keep up their run for about 15 feet (4.6 m) until they sink— then they use all four legs to break into a speedy swim.

SAY WHAT?!

BASILISK LIZARDS RUN UP TO FIVE FEET (1.5 M) A SECOND.

SAY WHAT?!

THEY CAN SWIM UNDERWATER FOR UP TO 30 MINUTES.

Basilisks can RUN ON WATER from the MOMENT they are BORN.

CAN TAKING PHOTOS OF WILD ANIMALS HELP SAVE THEM?

Q&A WITH PHOTOGRAPHER THOMAS NICOLON

Q: WHY IS IT IMPORTANT TO TAKE PHOTOS OF ANIMALS IN THE WILD?

A: When you photograph animals in their habitat, you are showing their behavior without interference, and that can be important information for scientists about things like how and where a species hunts.

Q: HOW CAN PHOTOGRAPHING ENDANGERED ANIMALS HELP PROTECT THEM?

A: Photos travel around the world. Take bonobos—bonobos are as close to humans as chimps are, but people don't know much about them. It's important to show the world what these animals look like and to learn why it is important to save them.

Q: DO YOU EVER GET SCARED OF THE ANIMALS YOU PHOTOGRAPH?

A: I do! I once got charged by a forest elephant and I had to run for my life, and when I stopped running, I was shaking. You must always keep in mind that we are in their home.

Q: WHAT ABOUT TAKING PHOTOS OF WILDLIFE IN MY NEIGHBORHOOD?

A: If you're quiet, you can get quite close to wildlife to observe them and take a photo. We see animals all the time, and we forget they're cool—like insects and birds and snakes. Try to capture their beauty.

BONUS!

How to Take Wild Photos of Your Pet

- Get down to your pet's eye level and try to snap a picture when they don't know you're watching.

- Get up close on a macro level—of, say, your dog's nose—to capture a new perspective.

- Don't be afraid of a blurry shot. Catch your pet in motion streaking across a room.

French wildlife photographer and National Geographic Explorer **Thomas Nicolon** travels around the world taking photos of wildlife—not only to capture beautiful images, but also to shed light on the animals' behavior, habitat, and struggles to survive because of environmental threats.

WHY do some ANIMALS have such BIG EARS?

Some animals' ears are their statement piece. The African elephant has the biggest ears of any animal on Earth. And believe it or not, these oversize ears help them keep cool. When it's hot, elephants radiate heat from blood vessels by increasing the blood supply to their ears. Elephants also flap their ears to generate a cool breeze, like a natural fan. Many types of animals similarly evolved oversize ears to help keep them cool in hot environments. Others use theirs to help detect prey. Bat-eared foxes use their giant ears to find underground termite colonies, their main source of food. Fennec foxes' ears serve multiple purposes: They help get rid of body heat in the foxes' North African habitat, and they allow them to find prey burrowed in the desert sand.

Fennec fox

ASIAN ELEPHANTS HAVE SMALLER EARS THAN THEIR AFRICAN COUSINS BECAUSE THEY LIVE IN SHADY RAINFORESTS.

CARACALS, a type of wild cat, have TUFTS on the TIPS of their oversize EARS, which may FUNNEL SOUND to locate prey.

How Animals Take the Heat

Where most animals would die, a few creatures thrive. These animals have adapted to survive in some of the hottest places on Earth.

DESERT SNAILS

To survive the intense heat and long dry spells of the Sahara, these snails close themselves up in their shells to maintain their moisture. They can remain dormant—for years, if necessary—until the rain comes, and then they revive.

POMPEII WORMS

These five-inch (13-cm)-long worms can take more heat than almost any other animal. They live next to deep-sea hydrothermal vents in temperatures almost hot enough to boil water.

PUPFISH

Just about an inch (2.5 cm) long, the pupfish is a survivor. Found in the Americas and the Caribbean, it can live in salt water that's three times saltier than the ocean! It has also been found in 100°F (38°C) hot spring waters in California and Nevada's Death Valley National Park.

CAN some ANIMALS TURN their HEADS all the way AROUND?

Almost. Owls can turn their heads better than any other animal on the planet. Unlike humans, whose eyes rotate in their eye sockets, owls' eyes are fixed. They have to stretch their necks to see what's around them. Owls can turn their heads in a half circle, about 180 degrees to the left or the right. This allows them to see everything around them, if they look both directions. Some owls, such as the barred owl, can even turn their heads as much as 270 degrees, or three-quarters of the way around. That's twice what humans can do! In addition to their excellent turning range, owls have flexible tissue and blood vessels, so this nimble move doesn't cause neck ache. Being able to see from all sides has a serious survival advantage: Owls can look over their shoulders to see a predator coming or to detect prey.

THANKS TO 17 NECK BONES, AN OSTRICH CAN EASILY TURN ITS NECK TO SEE WHAT IS HAPPENING BEHIND IT.

Like owls, the TARSIER—a primate—has EYEBALLS that CAN'T MOVE, but it can TURN ITS HEAD in a HALF CIRCLE.

SAY WHAT?!

PRAYING MANTISES CAN ROTATE THEIR TRIANGULAR HEADS 180 DEGREES TO SCAN THEIR SURROUNDINGS.

WHY do ANTEATERS have such long TONGUES?

Giant anteaters have two-foot (0.6-m)-long tongues—that's the longest tongue compared to body size of any animal. If an adult human had a tongue that was the same proportional length, it would hang down to their belly button! Anteaters don't have teeth, so their tongues have to do all the work to eat their food. And work it does. Giant anteaters can lap up 35,000 ants and termites in a day. Here's how they do it: Anteaters have an excellent sense of smell— about 40 times better than ours. Once they find an anthill or termite nest, they use their long, sharp claws to tear it open, and then they stick their long noses in. They quickly flick their tongues, which are covered in sticky saliva, up to 150 times a minute. This lets them capture and eat insects by the thousands.

A BABY ANTEATER HITCHES A RIDE ON ITS MOM'S BACK FOR ITS FIRST YEAR OF LIFE.

WHY do ARMADILLOS ROLL UP into a BALL?

Sometimes the best way to avoid conflict is to curl up into a ball. That's the approach of the three-banded armadillo, the only type of armadillo that can tuck itself away from danger. Named for the number of movable bands on their outer shells, these mammals from South America have body armor that shields them from predators and the thorny vegetation they walk through. When frightened or under attack, they protect their soft bellies by pulling in their legs and curling up into a ball. Though tucked tight, three-banded armadillos often leave a small space open. But if a predator tries to stick its nose or a paw through, the armadillo slams its armor completely closed as a reminder that it means business.

Armadillo means "LITTLE ARMORED ONE" in Spanish.

WHAT do BIRDS have in common with DINOSAURS?

Zhenyuanlong

Prepare to have your mind blown: Birds are dinosaurs. More specifically, they are descendants of theropods, a type of meat-eating dinosaur. (Theropods include *Tyrannosaurus rex* and velociraptors.) We know that 66 million years ago, an asteroid hit Earth, wiping out nearly all dinosaurs. But one group survived—avian dinosaurs. These dinosaurs were no bigger than ducks, and they adapted well to this catastrophic change. They didn't need to eat as much as their larger dinosaur relatives, and they were willing to eat just about everything—from seeds to fruit to insects to fish. Like many dinosaurs, avian dinosaurs had feathers. And they flew, which meant they could escape bad living conditions and travel to better food sources. That's why today, these avian dinosaurs, which we now call birds, are anything but extinct. They live on every continent on the planet, and come in hundreds of shapes and sizes.

PTEROSAURS **WERE THE** LARGEST ANIMALS EVER **TO** TAKE TO THE SKIES.

Researchers think DINOSAURS performed DISPLAY DANCES JUST AS BIRDS do today.

PTEROSAURS **LIVED AT THE** SAME TIME AS DINOSAURS, BUT THEY WEREN'T BIRDS OR DINOSAURS—THEY WERE REPTILES.

WHY do OPOSSUMS PLAY DEAD?

Opossums are good at make-believe. In fact, their theatrical stunt is so famous that it's become an expression: "playing possum." Opossums pretend to be dead, hoping that their dramatic trick is convincing enough that predators will move along and leave them alone. When under attack by a fox, bobcat, dog, or other predator, these little marsupials flop over on their sides, stick out their tongues, and stare straight ahead. They even emit a foul odor, and their heart rate slows. This can make predators suspicious and confused, giving opossums some time to escape. Playing possum is usually a tactic used by young opossums, which are less capable of holding their own when under attack. Adults tend to fight back: They bare their teeth, hiss, and screech.

Animal Tricksters

"Ssstay away. If I feel threatened, I play dead by flipping over on my back and opening my mouth wide. And if that's not enough to say 'do not disturb,' I flare my neck, pretending to be something much scarier than me: a cobra."

Hognose snake

Opossums can PLAY DEAD for a FEW MINUTES or UP TO SIX HOURS.

"I don't play dead to escape predators; I play dead to eat them. I'm willing to sink to the bottom of lakes in East Africa, lie on my side, and wait for scavenging fish to come by and investigate. When they do, I spring to life and, if I'm quick enough, grab a meal."

Cichlid fish

"Playing dead takes patience! If I get snatched and then dropped by a bird, I stay perfectly frozen—for up to an hour! Scurrying away would only draw attention. Keeping calm is my key to survival."

European antlion

NEWBORN OPOSSUMS ARE THE SIZE OF HONEYBEES.

HOW do CHEETAHS RUN SO FAST?

Cheetahs are the fastest land animals on Earth, able to reach speeds of up to 69.5 miles an hour (112 km/h). That's as fast as a car travels on a highway! And scientists have uncovered how these spotted speedsters are able to live life in the fast lane. A cheetah's spine is longer and more flexible than any of the other big cats' spines. When it sprints, its spine bunches and opens like a spring. This allows the cat's shoulders and hips to swing in arcs, maximizing each stride. Cheetahs can cover 30 feet (9 m) in one stride—that's the length of two medium-size cars! But when they run, it's almost never in a straight line. Their prey, like gazelles, run in a zigzag, and cheetahs follow their every move when on the chase. They use their long tails like rudders to help them counterbalance the twists and turns.

A cheetah's LEG and BACK MUSCLES make up HALF its BODY WEIGHT.

WHY do DOLPHINS JUMP OUT of the WATER?

For starters, dolphins know how to have a good time. They swim through the water at speeds of more than 18 miles an hour (29 km/h), playfully leaping as high as 20 feet (6 m) in the air. They also slap their tails on the water's surface, blow bubbles, and even butt heads with one another. Some dolphins swim beside ships; it's called bow riding, and some scientists think they do this to conserve energy. Spinner dolphins not only leap into the air, but also spin several times before landing back in the water. Scientists think this leaping and spinning helps get rid of fish that latch on to them and eat their parasites. And there may be one other purpose. Dolphins are extremely social and travel together in pods. Jumping could be a way of communicating messages like "Let's go!" and "Danger!"

A dolphin EATS FISH HEADFIRST so the SPINES DON'T GET CAUGHT in its THROAT.

WHAT's the MOST VENOMOUS FISH?

The world's most venomous fish looks anything but dangerous. Stonefish, which live in the shallow waters of northern Australia, are slow-moving, with flat heads, small eyes, and bumpy, algae-covered skin. And, as their name suggests, they look like stones! This allows them to camouflage in their rocky, coral habitat. But don't underestimate them. Stonefish have sharp dorsal fin spines that normally lie flat, but when the fish are disturbed, the spines pop up and inject venom into whatever has attacked them. The venom is stored in two sacs at the base of each spine, and the more venom that is released, the worse for their victim. If people accidentally step on a stonefish when swimming near the shore, it usually results in pain and swelling. An antivenom has also been developed, and deaths are rare. But the venom can be deadly to sea creatures.

STONEFISH DON'T USE THEIR VENOM TO ATTACK PREY— THEY ONLY USE IT IN DEFENSE.

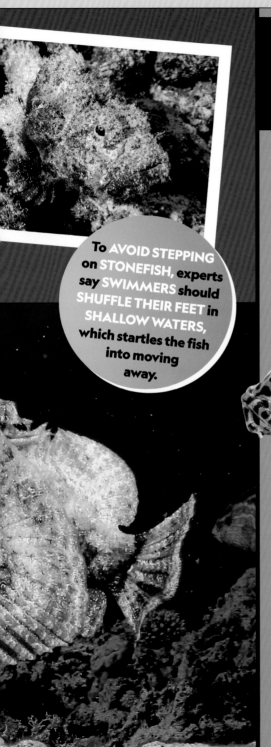

To **AVOID STEPPING on STONEFISH, experts** say **SWIMMERS should SHUFFLE THEIR FEET in SHALLOW WATERS,** which startles the fish into moving away.

Venomous or Poisonous:
What's the Difference?

It has to do with how the animals deliver their poison. Poisonous animals—like dart frogs and pufferfish—transfer their toxin through their skin or internal organs or the like when they are touched or eaten. Venomous animals—like snakes, scorpions, and bees—inject their toxin through stingers, spines, or fangs. Poisonous animals use their toxin to defend themselves from an attack. Venomous animals use their venom in both defense and to attack their prey. Animals can deliver their toxin a third way, too: Instead of covering themselves in poison or injecting it, some animals, including bombardier beetles and fire salamanders, spray poison at attackers, protecting themselves from a distance. But whether venomous or poisonous, these toxic animals can pack a dangerous punch.

Strawberry poison dart frog

King cobra

WHAT
IN THE WORLD?

A **group of zebras** is called a **dazzle**.

Plains zebras bark like a dog.

Each zebra has a **unique stripe pattern,** which may help them **recognize one another.**

ZEBRAS

WHY do KOALAS HUG TREES?

Koalas are serious tree huggers. After all, trees are where they eat, sleep, and lounge during the day. Koalas, which live in eucalyptus forests of southeastern and eastern Australia, eat more than a pound (.45 kg) of eucalyptus leaves every day. They spend so much time eating eucalyptus that they smell like it, too! The leaves have little nutritional value and take a long time to digest, so koalas don't have a lot of energy—which is why they sleep about 18 hours a day. They don't need to worry about water—they get most of their moisture from leaves. Trees also help them regulate their body temperature. A study found that in warm weather, koalas move to the lower, cooler parts of the trees and press their bodies close to the tree—their own kind of tree hug—to cool off. On colder days, koalas tend to rest farther away from the trunk where they can absorb heat in a sunspot.

KOALAS AREN'T BEARS. THEY ARE MARSUPIALS— FEMALES CARRY THEIR BABIES IN A POUCH.

SAY WHAT?!

A KOALA'S FIRST AND SECOND CLAWED TOES ARE FUSED TOGETHER, AND THE KOALA USES THEM LIKE A COMB.

Koalas' FINGERPRINTS look just like HUMAN fingerprints!

WHY does my CAT RUB against my LEGS?

Generally, cats aren't as obvious about their affection as dogs. When your kitty bumps into you, he's saying he likes you. But his nudge means other things, too. When cats rub up against you, or rub their cheeks on the furniture, they are marking their territory. Cats have scent glands in their cheeks, on their heads, and around their mouths that release a chemical that we can't see or smell but that other animals can detect. This form of marking tells other animals that you and everything else your kitty rubs is his. But rubbing and scent marking can also be a form of self-comfort for your cat. If he accidentally gets stuck in a closet, when you open the door you may find him heading straight to your legs to rub his cheek. This is his way of making himself feel better.

All in the Family

In many ways, big cats are just big kitties. Find out how similar domestic cats are to their big cat cousins.

DOMESTIC CATS

BIG CATS

RETRACTABLE CLAWS?

YES

YES, except for cheetahs

PURRS?

YES

YES, but only snow leopards, cougars, and cheetahs

RUBS ITS CHEEKS TO CLAIM TERRITORY?

YES

YES

SCRATCHES TREES TO CLAIM TERRITORY?

YES, and when inside, they scratch furniture

YES

SCRATCHY, SANDPAPER-LIKE TONGUE?

YES

YES

COUGHS UP HAIR BALLS?

YES

RARELY

HOW do BATS FLY in the DARK?

The world's smallest bat, the **BUMBLEBEE BAT,** WEIGHS LESS than a PENNY.

Most bats are nocturnal—they are most active at night—so being able to navigate in the dark is a very important skill. Bats use echolocation not only to find food but also to find their way around caves and other objects while they are flying. Here's how it works: Bats send out high-pitched sound waves that bounce off the objects around them and back to the bat. This tells them where and how big an object is. Echolocation is so accurate that bats can pinpoint the tiniest things, such as mosquitoes and the other insects they eat. But not all bats rely on echolocation to get around. A few species, like fruit bats, rely instead on their vision and sense of smell to find their food, which, as their name suggests, includes fruit and nectar.

WHY can't PENGUINS FLY?

Penguins' bodies are built to sail through the seas, not the sky. These barrel-shaped birds have evolved wings that work more like flippers, helping them swim and steer in the ocean. In fact, their wing bones are straight and unable to fold like most bird wings. And their body resembles a sea animal's more than a bird's. They have fat supplies, heavy muscles, and densely packed feathers that help them stay warm in cold water. One way penguins do "fly" is when they pop out of water and onto land or ice. Penguins' feathers collect little bubbles that create a layer of air around them, giving the birds extra speed and lift to sail out of the water as if they are flying—at least for a moment. Scientists think that, without these bubbles, the birds would struggle to get out of the water, which would be dangerous when the animals are trying to escape predators, like leopard seals.

ADÉLIE PENGUINS CAN LEAP UP TO 10 FEET (3 M) FROM THE WATER TO LAND.

DO all SPIDERS SPIN WEBS?

All spiders make silk, but not all spiders spin webs. A spider's silk is multipurpose: It helps a spider climb, works like a harness to keep a spider from falling, helps create egg sacs, catches and wraps up prey, and more.

Although many spiders build webs to trap insects and other animals, some, like crab spiders, skip the web and ambush prey that walks by. Jumping spiders stalk their prey and jump on it when they are ready to attack. Pirate spiders hang out on other spiders' webs, and when the web's owner comes to investigate, the pirate spider attacks it. Some young spiders use silk as a parachute of sorts. They climb to a high point, tilt their abdomen to the sky, and pull out some thread. The thread carries the spider to a new location. The diving bell spider perhaps has the most inventive use of silk: It builds a dome-shaped web underwater between plants, trapping air bubbles inside so that it can breathe inside its new home.

Garden orb weaver spider

DIVING BELL SPIDERS SPEND THEIR ENTIRE LIFE UNDERWATER.

168

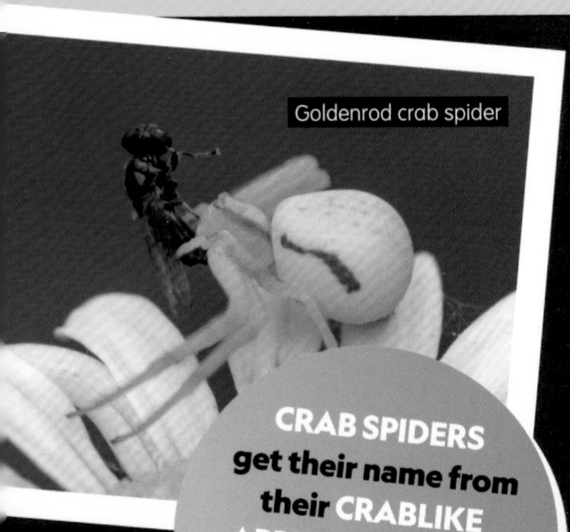

Goldenrod crab spider

CRAB SPIDERS get their name from their CRABLIKE APPEARANCE, and also their ability to WALK SIDEWAYS.

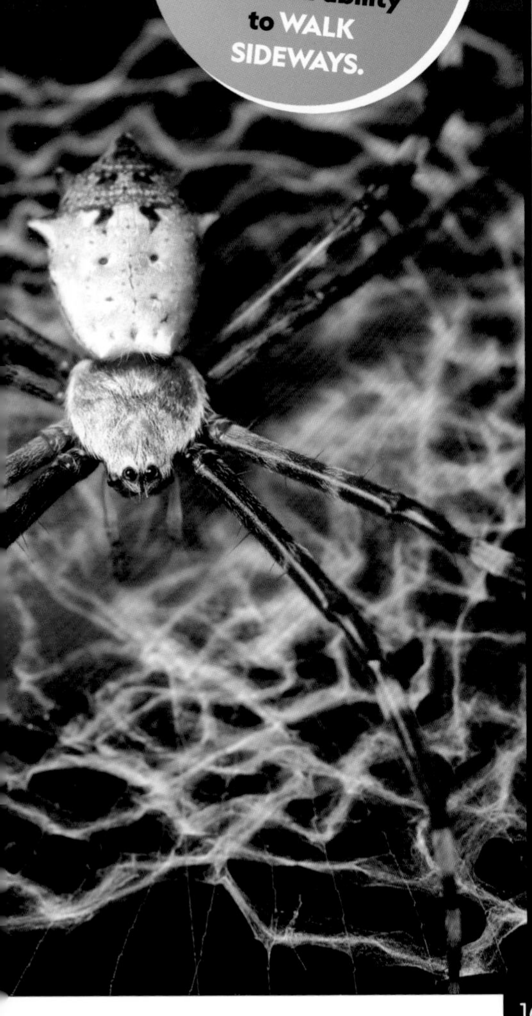

Do You Have a Spidey Sense?

Test your spider knowledge:

1. True or false: Spiders are insects.

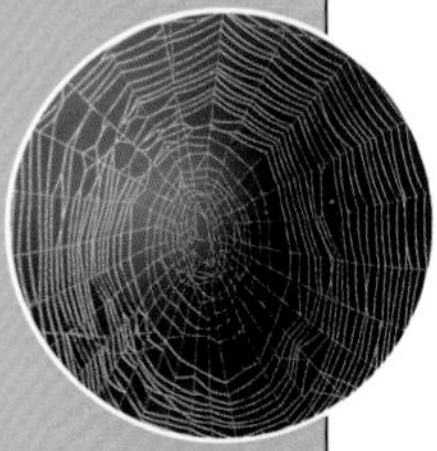

2. Ounce for ounce, spider silk is stronger than ___ .

a. string
b. a rubber band
c. a pencil
d. steel

3. A female black widow spider's red mark on her abdomen is shaped like a(n) _____ .

a. diamond
b. hourglass
c. triangle
d. heart

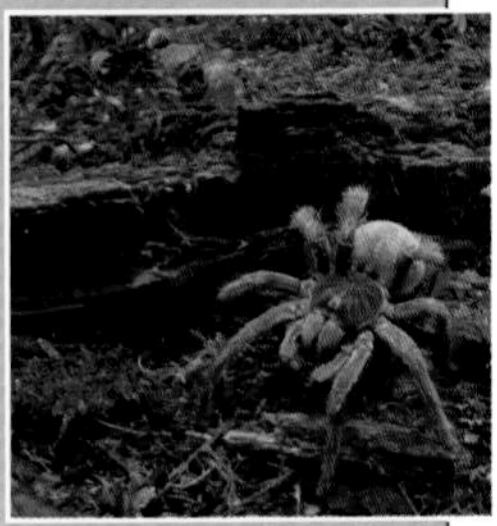

4. The Goliath birdeater spider has a leg span as wide as a ___ .

a. golf ball
b. tennis ball
c. softball
d. basketball

5. Wolf spiders get their name because they _____ .

a. are furry like a wolf
b. chase and pounce on prey like a wolf
c. travel in packs
d. howl

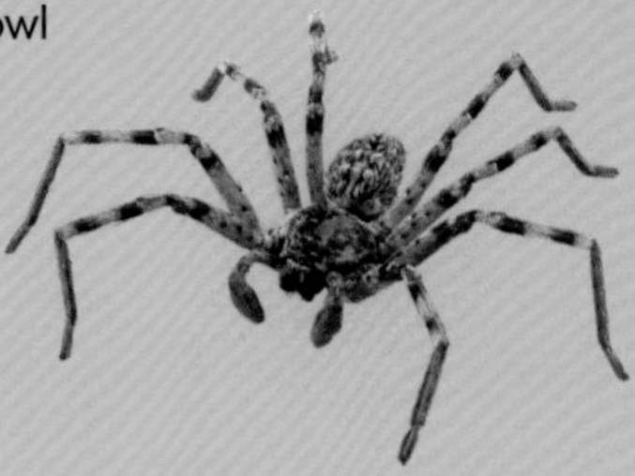

Answers: 1. False (They are arachnids.); 2. d; 3. b; 4. d; 5. b

WHY are COWS always CHEWING?

If you've ever watched a cow hang out in a pasture, chances are, it was chewing. Cows chew their cud almost eight hours a day, making their grand total of daily chews about 30,000! They are chewing on regurgitated food—food they ate once and brought back up to chew and swallow again. Yum! This regurgitated food is called cud. When a cow first eats its food, it just moistens it with saliva and then swallows it. Then bacteria go to work to soften the food, turning it into cud. The cud is brought back up to the cow's mouth, where the cow chews on it again. The cow's mouth generates saliva, which helps with the digestion process. A chewing cow is a healthy and relaxed cow. Cows that don't chew their cud tend to have poor quality milk and can have digestion and health issues.

COWS STAND UP AND LIE DOWN 16 TIMES A DAY, ON AVERAGE.

A cow produces about 60 POUNDS (27 kg) of POOP a DAY—that's the weight of a Labrador retriever.

THE MAIN STOMACH OF A COW HOLDS 40 GALLONS (151 L) OF FOOD—ENOUGH TO FILL A BATHTUB!

WHY do DOLPHINS come to the RESCUE?

Accounts as far back as ancient Greece detail dolphins coming to the rescue, saving humans from nearly drowning by helping them to shore. In 2004, four lifeguards in New Zealand were doing a training swim in the ocean when a pod of dolphins encircled them, frantically slapping the water with their fins. The lifeguards didn't know what the dolphins were doing until they spotted a great white shark just a few yards away. The dolphins maintained their protective ring for more than 30 minutes until the shark left. Do dolphins know what lifesavers they can be? There isn't scientific evidence to support such knowledge, but the people who lived to tell the tale might suggest otherwise.

DOLPHINS HAVE UNIQUE WHISTLES—LIKE NAMES—FOR EACH OTHER.

Dolphins SOMETIMES CATCH FISH by WHACKING them with their TAILS to STUN THEM.

Dogs to the Rescue

Dolphins aren't the only animal heroes. Some dogs are trained to be professional helpers.

ARSON DOGS

Arson dogs have a nose for fire. These canines help fire investigators figure out if a fire was an accident or set intentionally. They can smell chemicals used to start fires and then alert their human handler if they've found something.

EARTHQUAKE RESCUE DOGS

When a 7.1 earthquake shook Mexico City in 2017, Frida, a yellow Labrador retriever, came to the rescue. Frida and other rescue dogs led their handlers to where people were buried under rubble so rescuers could help free them.

AVALANCHE RESCUE DOGS

An avalanche can hit at any time, potentially burying skiers and anyone else in its way. Rescue dogs gather a scent and pinpoint where the person is buried. It takes 400 ski patrollers three days to do the work that an avalanche rescue dog can do in 20 minutes.

HOW do POLAR BEARS STAY WARM?

Most polar bears live within the Arctic Circle, where winter temperatures dip to minus 50°F (-46°C). But these mammals are built for the cold. A polar bear's coat not only helps it blend in with its snowy environment—it also keeps the bear warm. The dense undercoat and hollow hairs, which trap air, keep the bear insulated when it swims. Even though the fur looks white to our eyes, it is actually transparent and reflects visible light. A polar bear's skin is black, which helps absorb heat to keep it warm. But the bear's best defense in the cold climate is a layer of fat under its skin, which can be up to 4.5 inches (11 cm) thick! It acts as a wet suit and keeps the bear toasty. On cold, windy days on land, polar bears rely on more than their coat, skin, and fat to stay safe: They dig a shelter in a snowbank and curl up, covering their muzzle to stay warm.

POLAR BEARS CAN SWIM FOR DAYS AT A TIME.

Polar bears ROLL around in the SNOW to CLEAN THEIR COAT.

THEY HAVE FUR ON THE BOTTOM OF THEIR PAWS TO PROTECT AGAINST THE ICE AND SNOW IN THEIR ARCTIC HOME.

ANIMAL APPETITES: WHAT'S ON THE MENU?

The food that different animals eat is as different as the animals themselves. Find out what and how much these animals eat. Spoiler: The smallest animals sometimes have the biggest appetites!

GRIZZLY BEAR

ON THE MENU: Insects, plants, roots, berries, nuts, fruit, small rodents, fish, dead animals, large animals as big as moose

A FULL PLATE: Grizzly bears eat up to 30 pounds (14 kg) of food a day.

HUMMINGBIRD

ON THE MENU: Nectar from flowers and feeders, as well as insects, beetles, ants, mosquitoes, and gnats

A FULL PLATE: Hummingbirds consume about half their body weight in food each day.

AFRICAN ELEPHANT

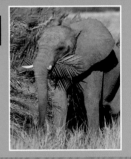

ON THE MENU: Roots, grass, fruit, and bark

A FULL PLATE: An adult elephant can eat up to 300 pounds (136 kg) of food in a single day.

GILA MONSTER

ON THE MENU: Birds' eggs, young birds, rodents, frogs, lizards, and insects

A FULL PLATE: A Gila monster—which can consume a third of its weight in one meal—needs to eat only three or four times a year.

LITTLE BROWN BAT

ON THE MENU: Mosquitoes, moths, and beetles

A FULL PLATE: Females eat up to 3,000 insects a night, which is 110 percent of their body weight.

DO FLYING SQUIRRELS really FLY?

Flying squirrels might not technically fly—bats are the only mammals capable of true flight—but they come close! Flying squirrels have a membrane that stretches along both sides of their body from their wrists to their ankles. When they leap from a tree branch, they pop open this membrane, which works like a built-in parachute. This lets them glide at distances up to 150 feet (46 m)—about half the length of a soccer field. Then they use their bushy tail to steer or slow down. Soaring through the air comes in handy when they are trying to escape predators like snakes, owls, and raccoons in forests.

FLYING SQUIRRELS are capable of making a 180-DEGREE TURN MIDAIR when being chased.

Soaring flying squirrel

More Wingless Animals That Go the Distance

Flying squirrels aren't the only animals with a trick up their sleeves. Here are some more creatures that take to the skies.

SUGAR GLIDER

This possum that can fit in the palm of your hand can glide the length of an Olympic-size pool. Like flying squirrels, these gliders have flaps of skin along their sides that give them lift. And as a marsupial, the mama sugar glider also has a pouch to carry her young.

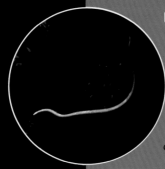

FLYING SNAKE

Despite their name, these snakes can't actually fly because they don't gain altitude. But they do free fall and contort their bodies to generate lift. They can even make turns! Flying snakes glide to escape predators and also to move from tree canopy to tree canopy.

WALLACE'S FLYING FROG

This frog species doesn't just hop. Wallace's flying frogs use membranes between their toes and loose flaps of skin along their sides to glide up to 50 feet (15 m) between tree branches in tropical jungles. They even have special pads that help them "stick" the landing on a jump.

ARE some FISH ELECTRIC?

Yes! And they don't need an outlet to keep themselves charged. Electric eels use their electrical charge to stun prey and keep predators away. They have electric organs with cells that store power like little batteries. To attack prey or respond to a threat, they discharge an electrical current of up to 600 volts—that's five times the power of a standard U.S. outlet. Even though these creatures are called electric eels, they aren't in the eel family. They are knifefish and are more closely related to carp and catfish. They are air breathers and need to surface frequently. But these eels aren't the only fish with shock value. Electric rays also generate electric shocks and can even control the voltage that their shock releases. To warn a predator to back off, they send out a low-level shock. To find dinner, they turn it up to a full charge.

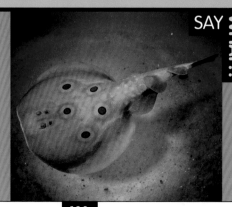

ANCIENT ROMANS AND GREEKS CALLED ELECTRIC RAYS "NUMBFISH," BELIEVING THE RAYS COULD RELIEVE PAIN IF THEY PUT THEM ON THEIR BODIES.

SAY WHAT?!

ELECTRIC EELS, WHICH LIVE IN STREAMS AND PONDS IN SOUTH AMERICA, GROW UP TO EIGHT FEET (2.4 M) LONG.

An electric eel's **THREE SPECIALIZED ELECTRIC ORGANS** take up 80 percent of its body.

WHY do PRAIRIE DOGS KISS NOSES?

What better way to greet a family member than to nuzzle them on the nose? Prairie dogs, a type of rodent that lives in underground burrows, say hello to fellow family members with a "kiss." They rub noses and teeth, which confirms that the prairie dogs are in the same family group. Prairie dogs have a tight bond. Families consist of a male, several females, and six or more young. They build and defend their burrow system, called a town, which consists of multiple rooms. They even have a designated spot for the bathroom! Intruders beware: Prairie dogs protect their burrows from black-footed ferrets—which try to break in to eat their favorite prey—by setting up listening posts at the entrance. Prairie dogs keep each other close, constantly reinforcing family bonds by "kissing," sharing food, grooming one another, and sitting side by side.

PRAIRIE DOGS CHOP DOWN ANY TALL GRASSES GROWING AROUND THEIR TOWN SO THEY CAN KEEP A BETTER LOOKOUT FOR PREDATORS.

Adorable Animal Behaviors

Prairie dogs win the prize for cutest meet-and-greet, but these animals also know how to bring the *aww*.

The LARGEST recorded PRAIRIE DOG TOWN was home to as many as 400 MILLION PRAIRIE DOGS.

VAMPIRE BATS SNUGGLE

Sure, they might be a little bloodthirsty, but vampire bats have a soft, cuddly side. Female vampire bats snuggle together to stay warm, and even groom each other and share food.

GIRAFFES HUM TO ONE ANOTHER AT NIGHT

Giraffes make ultralow sounds that humans can barely hear, but if that volume were turned up, we'd hear humming. Researchers discovered that giraffes hum to one another all night long. They don't know what the hums mean; perhaps it's a type of snoring or maybe it's one way the giraffes communicate with one another.

NURSE SHARKS NAP TOGETHER

Nurse sharks are nocturnal, so they spend their day sleeping. But unlike most sharks, nurse sharks make sleeping a group activity. Up to 40 sharks pile on the ocean floor in a big cuddle puddle.

INDEX

Boldface indicates illustrations.

INDEX

INDEX

Since 1888, the National Geographic Society has funded more than 14,000 research, conservation, education, and storytelling projects around the world. National Geographic Partners distributes a portion of the funds it receives from your purchase to National Geographic Society to support programs including the conservation of animals and their habitats. To learn more, visit natgeo.com/info.

For more information, visit national geographic.com, call 1-877-873-6846, or write to the following address:

National Geographic Partners, LLC
1145 17th Street NW
Washington, DC 20036-4688 U.S.A.

For librarians and teachers: national geographic.com/books/ librarians-and-educators

More for kids from National Geographic: natgeokids.com

National Geographic Kids magazine inspires children to explore their world with fun yet educational articles on animals, science, nature, and more. Using fresh storytelling and amazing photography, *Nat Geo Kids* shows kids ages 6 to 14 the fascinating truth about the world—and why they should care. **natgeo.com/subscribe**

For rights or permissions inquiries, please contact National Geographic Books Subsidiary Rights: bookrights@ natgeo.com

Designed by Amanda Larsen

Trade paperback
ISBN: 978-1-4263-7275-9
Reinforced library binding
ISBN: 978-1-4263-7264-3

The publisher would like to thank Julie Beer, author and researcher; Grace Hill Smith, project manager; Avery Naughton, project editor; Lori Epstein, photo editor; Robin Palmer, fact-checker; and Anne LeongSon and Gus Tello, associate designers.

Printed in China
22/RRDH/1

GOT MORE QUESTIONS?
WE'VE GOT ANSWERS!

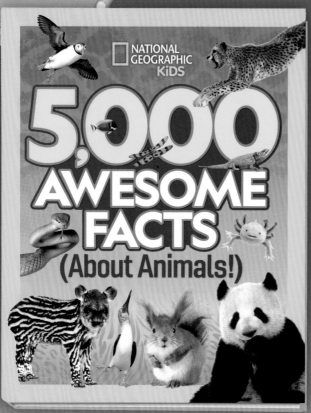

NATIONAL GEOGRAPHIC KiDS

5,000 AWESOME FACTS
(About Animals!)

Discover tons of facts about the thousands of animals that call Earth home in this oversized, fact-packed, photo-filled book.